# The Big Book of Raising Chickens for Beginners

A Practical Guide to Raise Healthy and Happy Backyard Herd for Meat and Eggs Plus Breeding, Routine Care and More

By

Zelene Ward

## Copyright © 2021 – Zelene Ward

## All rights reserved

No part of this publication may be reproduced, distributed, or transmitted in any form or by any means, including photocopying, recording, or other electronic or mechanical methods, without the prior written permission of the publisher, except in the case of brief quotations embodied in reviews and certain other non-commercial uses permitted by copyright law.

## Disclaimer

This publication is designed to provide competent and reliable information regarding the subject matter covered. However, the views expressed in this publication are those of the author alone, and should not be taken as expert instruction or professional advice. The reader is responsible for his or her own actions.

The author hereby disclaims any responsibility or liability whatsoever that is incurred from the use or application of the contents of this publication by the purchaser or reader. The purchaser or reader is hereby responsible for his or her own actions.

# Table of Contents

Introduction ............................................................................. 8

Chapter 1 ................................................................................ 10

Basics to Raising Chickens ................................................... 10

    Pros and Cons of Raising Chickens ................................. 10

    Chicken Behavior: Normal Vs. Abnormal ....................... 13

    Chicken Terminologies ...................................................... 18

    Popular Chicken Breeds .................................................... 24

    Choosing The Right Chicken Breed ................................. 35

Chapter 2 ................................................................................ 40

Buying Your Chickens ........................................................... 40

Chapter 3 ................................................................................ 48

Housing Your Chickens ......................................................... 48

    Chicken Housing Options ................................................ 49

        Free-Range Housing .................................................... 49
        Cages ............................................................................ 52
        Shelter and a Run ........................................................ 55

- Chicken Tractor ............................................................. 57
- Buy or Build a Chicken House? .................................... 61
- Building a Proper Chicken House ................................. 63
  - Size of the Coop ........................................................ 64
  - Location of the Coop ................................................ 65
  - Insulation of the Coop .............................................. 66
  - Cross-Ventilation ...................................................... 66
  - Storage Space ............................................................ 67
  - Nesting Boxes ............................................................ 67
  - Flooring ...................................................................... 68
  - Electricity ................................................................... 68
  - Temperature .............................................................. 69
  - Access to Feed and Water ........................................ 69
  - Roost ........................................................................... 69
  - Droppings Board ....................................................... 70
- Runs and Yards for Your Chickens ............................... 70
  - Confined Runs ........................................................... 71
  - Dust Bath .................................................................... 71
- Cleaning the Chicken Coop ............................................ 72
- Protecting Your Chickens From Predators .................. 73
- Chicken Mortality Management .................................... 78

# Chapter 4 ............................................................................ 85

# Feeding Your Chickens .................................................... 85

Chicken Feed Types ............................................................. 85

Feed for Chicks .................................................................. 89

Feed for Egg-Laying Hens ................................................. 89

Feed for Meat Chickens ..................................................... 90

Foods to Avoid .................................................................. 91

How Much Do I Feed? ...................................................... 94

Chicken Feeders and Waterers ......................................... 95

Chapter 5 ............................................................................... 107

Breeding Your Chickens ....................................................... 107

Implement a Breeding Plan ............................................. 108

Breeding Methods ............................................................ 109

Breeding Chickens For Egg Production ........................ 109

What to Feed Your Breeder Chickens ............................ 110

What to Feed Your Broody Hens .................................... 110

Incubation of Eggs ............................................................ 112

    Egg Selection ................................................................ 113
    Temperature and Humidity Control ....................... 115
    Cleaning Your Incubator ........................................... 116

Hatching Chicks ........................................................... 117

    Chick Hatching Process ........................................ 117
    What To Do With Your Hatched Chicks ............... 118
    Potential Chick Hatching Issues .......................... 119
    Keeping Records ................................................... 120
Likely Chicken Breeding Issues .................................. 120

Caring For Newborn Chicks ....................................... 123

Proper Handling of Eggs ............................................ 125

    Egg Cleaning and Handling ................................. 127
    Grading and Sorting Eggs ................................... 128
    Storage of Eggs .................................................... 130
    Requirements When Selling Eggs ....................... 131
    Cooking and Handling Egg Foods ...................... 132
Chapter 6 ..................................................................... 136

Raising, and Butchering Meat Chickens ................... 136

    Raising Meat Chickens ........................................ 137

    Selecting The Right Chickens ............................. 137
    Selecting The Best Time To Raise Chickens ....... 138
    Number of Chickens to Raise .............................. 138
Butchering Your Meat Chickens ................................ 140

    Are Your Chickens Ready? .................................. 140
    Get a Butcher or Do It Yourself .......................... 141
    Killing The Chicken ............................................. 141

Meat Collection, Cleaning, and Storage ............................ 145

Conclusion ............................................................................ 148

References ............................................................................ 149

# Introduction

Chickens are one of the friendliest and loveliest animals in the world, but sometimes, raising them may call for a deeper level of intricacy and meticulousness. Just like humans, they are susceptible to falling sick and even dying, but with the right care, you'd be able to scale through the hurdles. However, it gets all good the moment they begin to lay eggs for you. Meat is another lovely thing they could offer to your table, and not having to buy that in the market comes with a very exciting feeling. However, for a flawless trial, it is recommended that you understand the nooks and crannies of how to raise chickens for meat and egg production. That's why this book, ***The Big Book of Raising Chickens for Beginners*** was written. It encapsulates all the needed tips, and guidelines that you need for a successful journey in the poultry business. The concept of breeding, raising, feeding, housing, maintaining, caring, incubating, protecting, and managing chickens, and much more are all discussed. Each of these topics is packed with several nuggets that will no doubt get you hooked.

So, without further ado, let's delve right into the first thing you need to know as a beginner, the basics of raising chickens.

# Chapter 1

# Basics to Raising Chickens

Chickens are commonly known as domestic fowls. They are birds that exist as various species, with each one serving a different purpose. Some farmers raise them for eggs, meat, or both. There are several kinds of domestic fowls, and each of them has its uniqueness, both in the manner with which they grow and the kind of care that they need. Some require a raising period of a few months, and for some others, they could need tendering for years, but before we jump into anything deep about chickens, let's first discuss the basic information you need to know about raising birds.

## Pros and Cons of Raising Chickens

As a beginner, it is crucial to know the good and bad sides of chicken rearing. Such information would always guide you on what to do, and how to harness your skills to the maximum.

## Pros.

1. Raising chickens can be one very great source of income for you! You might not even need to have

a side job once you can get it kicking. You could sell the chicks, the eggs, the adult fowls, or even own an incubation business for large-scale farmers! You need not worry about a market as there's always a constant demand for them.
2. You need not worry about consuming stale farm products like eggs, or meat. As long as you have chickens in your yard, there's a free supply day in and day out. Also, since you are invariably responsible for their feeding, you can easily monitor what they eat and what they drink, to protect your health.
3. This is the business for you if you love the art of sole proprietorship. Chickens are small and so, you could easily manage to handle about a hundred of them without getting fatigued. You could even use the help of your family members if need be.
4. There are already processed chicken feeds everywhere you go, so you do not have to worry about having to feed processing.
5. Chickens will not pose any risk of attack to you.
6. If you are considering a large-scale farm production that covers both the raising of

chickens and the planting of crops, you wouldn't have to worry too much about manure. Their droppings are just the perfect choice for your soil fertilizing agents.
7. To raise chickens, you do not need to have any form of qualification or license! With the right determination and a vast area of land, you are good to go.
8. Chickens have beautiful looks that can in a way add to the beauty of your house. Besides, they also have soft and fluffy feathers that are nice to touch.

**Cons.**

1. Chickens pass out droppings almost all the time, so, you might have to do series of litter changes to prevent the buildup of pests and diseases.
2. Most of the geographical locations lack some of the essential equipment that is important for raising chickens. Some of these supplies include chicken feed, water troughs, feeding troughs, chicks, etc.
3. Having a skilled veterinarian at the beginning of this business is crucial as you might not

understand most of the behaviors displayed by the birds when they are sick. So, not being able to get a skilled person to attend to that area of the business could be quite a hassle.
4. If you have your business sited in areas where poultry is the norm of the day, you might have it difficult to get a proper and steady market for your products.
5. Chickens aren't particularly quiet animals, so there could be an issue if you have a neighbor that wants his peace.
6. Chickens are very prone to falling sick, and this can be very bad if they begin to die as a result.
7. At first, when you begin the business of poultry, you might have to incur a lot of expenses getting the required necessities.

**Chicken Behavior: Normal Vs. Abnormal**

If there's anything that you should know as a beginner, it would be the fact that chickens do not always jump around healthily. There are a few times they just lie at some lonely spots for days, or worse still, bury their heads inside the crook of their feathers. Here, we will look at a few tips that you could use to know when your fowls need care. First, it is important to know what behaviors are normal in chickens. Let's take a look at them.

1. Fights: Just like lizards compete for females, chickens also do too. The male fowls are usually the ones to fight when there's a female lurking around. Apart from that, they fight for food, and dominance that is meted out in some other areas. This attitude is completely normal, but the moment you notice it getting out of hand, it's time to meddle.
2. Mate: If you have ever caught sight of two fowls mating, you'd agree that it doesn't look fun at all. It usually starts with the male fowl doing a strange kind of dance in which one of its wings lowers to the ground. Then, it would make its move to the female hen by moving in a half-circle. If the female happens to at that time be inclined to its mating advances, she'd squat for him. But the other times, the male would just hop on her back and grip her neck pretty roughly with its beak. This act is indeed very normal.

3. Ground digging: When you see a fowl digging or scratching across the ground with its claws, it's not because they are sick. They do that when searching for food particles like tiny bugs, and plant roots.
4. A freeze in a bird's laying: Just like human beings, birds also get tired. They don't lay all the time. Most times, they stop during the winter or when they need to molt. Instead of injecting your birds with all sorts of injections, you could encourage them to lay by always providing them with light even after the sunsets. Sometimes, these birds stop laying so that they can grow out a new set of feathers. The only thing that you could do to aid their laying would be to feed them with the essential proteins and vitamins.
5. Crowing: Cocks have always been known to crow once morning breaks, and there is nothing anyone can do to stop that. It's an instinct for them, so, you might just have to let them grow. If you however cannot handle the noise, you could get the species that do not crow.
6. Preening: This term is a time when a fowl uses its beak as well as its tongue to get dirt and bug out

of its fluff of feathers. Sometimes, one could think them to be plucking their feathers out of the pores, but that's wrong.
7. Rolling in the sand: You might have seen fowls rustling their feathers and wings through the sandy soils. They do that to protect themselves from parasites like bugs that climb onto them. To them, it's something that fetches them relief, and yes, it is extremely normal.

Now, let us look at a few abnormal behaviors that a fowl could put up. These are usually the disturbing ones and you might need to pay more attention to them as a beginner.

1. Pecking and plucking of feathers: This issue arises when the fowls in a room are too crowded together. So, they end up pecking at each other's bodies or plumage. If the room is not crowded, then, it could only mean that the bird's just naturally destructive. In that case, culling the bird will help protect the others from following such a trend.
2. Cannibalism: Chickens tend to be natural cannibals. So, when they see dead chickens,

they'd just go ahead to eat it. As long as the dead chicken is not with a disease, they are seldom affected by it. However, the moment you catch one of your fowls killing and then, eating another fowl, it might be that they are too crowded together. To solve this issue, you might have to reduce the number of fowls in one compartment of the cage.

3. Incessant mating: This issue usually arises when there are too many male fowls in a cage. So, they tend to be overly aggressive while trying to mate the hen. Sometimes, after one is done, another would immediately climb on her back. If that was to continue for long, the hen might end up losing a majority of her feathers or dying, even. So, to solve this issue, ensure that you get rid of the excess males, or better still, introduce more hens to the flock.

4. Falling wings: When you see a chicken standing around a corner with the feathers pointing towards the floor in a kind of saggy manner, it could be that it is sick. This wing issue is one of the symptoms of a whole lot of diseases. Once you notice this, ensure that you separate it from

the others to avoid the risk of a general infection. Afterward, you could check it out for more symptoms that would help you treat it.

5. Dullness: Fowls love to move around the place, peck at soils, or scratch across the ground. The moment you notice a fowl lying down in a place for a long time without moving, then, you might need to treat it as there's a high possibility that it's sick.
6. Mating between two different chicken species: The moment you notice a male duck mating with your hen, it's time to have them live separately. The genital organs of a duck are not compatible with that of a hen, and so, much damage might be done to the hen afterward.

## Chicken Terminologies

As a beginner, you would hear several fowl-related words, and it's very crucial to understand a whole lot of them and what they mean.

1. Chick: A young fowl that just got hatched.
2. Cockerel: A male fowl that is not yet up to a year old.
3. Pullet: A female fowl that is not up to a year old.

4. Juvenile: A young male or female fowl.
5. Cock: A male fowl whose age is either one old or above.
6. Hen: A female fowl that is either one year old or above.
7. Rooster: A male hen.
8. Capon: A castrated male bird.
9. Bantam: this refers to the species of fowls with small sizes.
10. Layer breed: This is the species of fowl that is raised primarily for its egg.
11. Dual-purpose breed: This is the species of fowl that is raised primarily for both its egg and meat.
12. Ornamental breed: This is a species of fowl that is raised primarily for a show or an exhibition.
13. Production breed: This is a species of fowl that is raised for its high level of meat and egg production.
14. A nesting cubicle: This term refers to a pouch or box where a hen can lay her eggs.
15. Bedding: This term refers to the litter that is spread across the floor of a poultry house.

16. Hardware cloth: This term refers to the solid material with the structure of a net that keeps the fowls in a place.
17. Chicken wire: This is a netting style made with light wire strings and a hexagonal mesh.
18. Brooder: This is a small space where chicks are raised.
19. Roosting: This is a group of resting fowls.
20. Chicken tractor: This is a mobile fowl coop that doesn't have a floor.
21. Coop: This is a cage or confines where fowls are kept.
22. Run: This is fenced rangeland for your fowls.
23. Molting: This term refers to the loss of feathers by a bird when there's a change in the season.
24. Frizzle: This is a type of feather that a fowl possesses that's usually subject to curls.
25. Down: This is the mass of soft, fluffy, and light feathers that stays at the first layer of the fowl's skin.
26. Muff: This term refers to the bits of a feather that pop out of the face and neck of a fowl.
27. Saddle: This refers to the feathers that run out from the tail.

28. Beard: The mass of feathers under the beak that makes the fowl look bigger than it is.
29. Pin: This term refers to the feather that grows after molting.
30. Wryneck: This is a condition in which chicks suffer from Vitamin E deficiency. So, their necks get twisted, and they have trouble balancing themselves on their feet.
31. Amprolium: This term refers to a medication that cures coccidiosis.
32. Mites: These are pest-like bugs that live within the feathers of fowls.
33. Poultry lice: These lice live exclusively within chicken feathers.
34. Dust bath: This is a bath that a chicken can ruffle its feathers through to remove parasites from its feathers, and to manage its plumage.
35. Coccidiosis: This is a disease of the intestine where a microscopic parasite attaches itself to the intestinal lining of an organism.
36. Avian Influenza: This is a naturally occurring virus that is detrimental to the health of fowls.
37. Fowlpox: This is a disease caused by a virus that introduces lesions to their skin.

38. Newcastle disease: This is a disease that is highly contagious among birds.
39. Salmonella: A bacteria that lives within the intestine, and is tied to food poisoning.
40. Bumblefoot: An inflammation on the feet of birds.
41. Pasty butt: This term describes a condition in which the vent of a chicken gets clogged by its droppings.
42. Grower feed: This is a feed that contains all the necessary vitamins for a growing chick that falls within the range of 16 weeks.
43. Layer feed: This feed is great for hens that are laying eggs, as it helps to boost their egg production.
44. All flock feed: This feed is a general-purpose feed that works for all birds.
45. Gamebird feed: This is a feed with a high level of protein to enhance the growth of gamebirds.
46. Scratch: This is a mix of several grains like corn.
47. Grit: This refers to the tiny stones in the gizzard that helps a fowl crush its food.
48. Wattle: This refers to the flesh beneath the beak of a chicken that helps to regulate heat.

49. Crop: This is the stomach of a fowl where food is temporarily stored.
50. Cloaca: This is the opening through which a fowl defecates, urinates, and mates.
51. Spurs: This is one sharp appendage that grows on the legs of chickens.
52. Comb: This is the part of a fowl's head with no feathers.
53. Vent: An opening through which a hen lets out her egg.
54. Crest: This is the feather that pops out of a chicken's head.
55. Broody: This term refers to a chicken that sits on and hatches her eggs herself.
56. Bloom: This is the thin coating that covers an egg to protect it from bacterial infection.
57. Candle: This is a light that can be used to access the inside of an egg.
58. Internal pip: This is a term that relates to a chick breaching into the airbag of the egg during the hatching process.
59. External pip: This is a term that describes the first crack that a chick makes on the shell while breaking out.

60. A clutch: This is a group of about twelve to fifteen eggs that are placed together so that they can easily be hatched.
61. Blastoderm: This is a term used for fertile eggs.
62. Blastodisc: This is a term used for infertile eggs.
63. Incubator: This is a machine that helps to hatch eggs.

**Popular Chicken Breeds**

There are several kinds of species of chickens out there, and each of them is usually raised for specific reasons, which will be discussed subsequently.

1. The Orpington Chicken

- This chicken is a very common breed.
- They are known as pure breeds.
- It is a dual-purpose chicken, i.e., it supplies both eggs and meat.
- They are resistant to harsh weather conditions.
- In a year, this breed can lay about two hundred eggs. The eggs are usually light brown.
- They have single, red and serrated combs with an elongated wattle.
- They have small and red earlobes with featherless legs.
- The darkly colored birds have dark eyes, but the light-colored ones have red eyes.
- A few species of this fowl produce pink-colored eggs.
- They like to wander about in search of insects.
- This chicken is extremely fluffy.

2. Wyandotte Chicken

- This breed is another popular breed.
- Their feathers have varieties of colors that cover gold, white, black, blue, and silver.
- They have yellow skins.
- Their colored feathers make them good for shows.
- They have risen combs, red earlobes, and red wattles.
- They have featherless legs with four toes.
- They like to fly, so, you might want to have their wings clipped.
- The males are pretty aggressive.
- They are sensitive to excessive sunlight.

- This fowl is a dual-purpose bird.
- It lays approximately two hundred eggs per year.
- This chicken is great for your backyard.

3. Plymouth Rock Chicken

- This breed is a wonderful breed for beginners.
- They are dual-purpose in nature, egg and meat.
- They are calm, docile, and free to move about.
- They are exceptional layers that give about 280 eggs per year.

4. Australorp Chicken

- A dual-purpose breed.
- A great choice for beginners.
- They have nice plumage and egg-laying abilities.

5. Brahma Chicken

- This chicken weighs about 16.5 pounds, and that is a bit heavier than the weight of an average fowl.
- They have a rather threatening look; however, they are indeed caring.
- They perform excellently in a cold climate.
- They lay about 150 eggs per year.
- This fowl is majorly cultivated for its meat.
- They are usually referred to as the King of Chickens because of their size.

- They come in different colors.
- They have red eyes, with a small and single pea-comb.
- They have feathers on their legs.
- They are submissive birds.
- They mature within two years.
- They don't fly.

6. Leghorn Chicken

- They are excellent layer breeds that lay about 280 eggs per year.
- They can fly easily.
- This fowl is relatively restless.

- They do well in warm climates since they have a large comb, and light build.

7. Rhode Island Red

- This is a bird ideal for beginners.
- They are calm and docile birds.
- They are good layers that can lay about 280-300 large eggs per year.
- They have yellow skin.
- They have a single comb with broad extensions.
- They have a clean leg.

- Long exposure to the sun usually causes the colors of their feathers to fade.
8. Silkie Chicken

- These birds originated in China
- Their feathers lack barbicels, and that explains their fluffy appearance.
- They have a topknot—a poof of feathers that sits on their head.
- Their faces are entirely covered with feathers.
- There are several colors in which this chicken comes in—red, buff, white, and black.
- They have blue or turquoise earlobes.
- They have brown or black eyes.

- The walnut-shaped comb is a thick piece of skin that is either red or purple.
- The hens and the roosters are known for their high levels of protectiveness.
- They have fluffy and puffy feathers.
- They can be great pets for kids.
- They are docile, sweet, and loving.
- They are good choices for your backyard.

9. Cochin Chicken

- These fowls have their legs are covered with a lot of feathers.
- They are big with a beautiful appearance, and so, can be used as an ornamental bird.
- They have feathers on their feet.

- They are easy to control.
- The hen is a great mother that even fosters the chicks of other breeds.
- You might not be able to easily lift this chicken.
- They are great for shows and exhibitions.

10. Cemani Chicken

- This is an exotic breed of chicken.
- They have one color of feather and the color is usually solid.
- They aren't the kind of birds that can be cuddled, but you could sit them in your laps.
- They are pretty expensive.

## Choosing The Right Chicken Breed

Do you want to raise chickens for eggs or meat or both? Or do you want to raise them for ornamental purposes? What chicken breed would suit your purpose best? Here, we will study a few tips that will guide you in choosing the right chicken breed.

- **What purpose do you want to raise fowls for?**

    As discussed earlier, there are several breeds of chicken one could choose from. But then, each of them is good for one thing or the other. For example, the fowls that are great for meat production usually would grow very fast. Some of them include the following;

    - Jersey Giant.
    - Brahma
    - Red Ranger
    - Cornish Cross.
    - Freedom Ranger.

    For egg production, you might want to choose any of the following breeds;

    - Rhode Island Red
    - Hamburg

- Campine
- Red Star
- Black Star
- Plymouth Rock chickens
- Golden Comet.

For both egg and meat production, you might want to choose from the following breeds;

- Plymouth Rock
- Wyandotte
- Sussex
- Rhode Island Red
- New Hampshire Red
- Buff Orpington.

For pets, you can work with the Bantam chicken breed. They are docile and loving animals.

For entertainment purposes, i.e., fights, you could go for any of the following;

- Asil
- Modern Game
- Old English Game
- American Game Bantam Chicken.

- **Your way of living**

    This section is where you table out how much time you have to spare for your poultry business. Fowls are animals that usually require a lot of care and attention, so, you might want to take time knowing what you want to choose. If you aren't going into this full-time, you should probably go for a species that is inexpensive and easy to manage. You can choose the ones that require more attention if you have much time to spare.

- **How much space do you have for your poultry business?**

    Fowls are just like birds that always want to roam all over the place. So, you have to ensure that you some free space for raising your chickens. The fewer chickens you need, the lesser the space you need. But then, if you are going for many, you might need to invest in a large space.

- **What is the weather condition like in your area?**

    You should take note of how the weather is in your area before choosing the kind of breed to raise. Some fowls cannot withstand cold temperatures, so, if you live in areas with constant storms and rain, you might want to go for fowls with proper feather adaptations. Some other breeds can survive in both cold and hot climates though.

- **What's your plumage choice?**

    There are several colors of plumage available, and they include black, buff, blue, white, and different tones of brown. Choose the one that suits your taste the best.

- **What color of eggs do you prefer?**

    The different egg colors available include blue, dark brown, pink, cream, olive, or tinted eggs. Some breeds like Cream Legbar, Easter Egger chickens, and Ameraucanas lay blue eggs.

Generally, as a beginner, you might want to ensure that all the birds in your flock fall into the same age range so that you can keep things simple and easy to manage.

You should also probably start with the same breeds as each breed of fowl have their time range for growth and development. If some grow very big, the stronger ones could fight and kill the weaker or smaller ones. Then, lastly, start on a small scale first, get used to the system of poultry, and then you can add more to your flock.

## Chapter 2

## Buying Your Chickens

After choosing the breed you want, the next thing you need to do is buy them. As a beginner, you also need to prioritize what you are buying. You don't want to buy chicks that'd just die a day after you get them. The meticulousness of the whole process increases when you decide to buy chickens that are a few weeks or months old. So, here, a few tips will be dropped on what you need to look out for when buying your first set of chickens.

- **Do I start with hatching chicks or older chickens?**

    This is the very question that most people tend to neglect. The other times, they just ignore the importance of it altogether, and usually, at the end of the day, they'd come to realize the mistake in their decisions. When starting a poultry business, you should start with the young chicks, that is, the newly hatched ones. Why? because you'd be able to ensure that they get all the necessary medication and minerals. How healthy a fowl will be at its latter stages depends heavily on the foundational things you supply it with. There are also other advantages attached to this choice, and they include the following;

- You can have access to a wide range of fowl species.
- The chicks can be gotten at a price that is least expensive when compared to the adult fowls.
- You could raise the chicks using the style you want.
- If you want friendly chickens, you might want to start raising them yourself.

Even with these many options, buying a chicken that is a few months old is the rather safer option for a beginner. For instance, if you are going into the raising of some breeds that require intensive care and monitoring at their early life stage, you might need to have a bit of know-how on these things—brooding, and medication dispensing. So, to prevent failed trials, you could just purchase your birds from a well-trusted and skilled farmer. The other reasons attached to this option include the following:

- They are less prone to diseases.
- The adult chickens get to lay quicker.
- The older chickens require less attention than the younger ones.
- With this technique, you could pick out what gender of species you want—male or female. It's not usually clear when they are in the 'chick' form.

- **Where to buy your chickens**

There are several places where you can get your chickens, but one thing remains crucial if you are getting the older ones—you getting a reliable and skilled farmer that has armed the chicks with all the necessary medication and the right feeding. For younger ones, try the following options;

- The feed store.
- The hatchery sites.
- Online farmer groups.

When purchasing your fowls online, you might need to be very careful. Ensure that the store allows a return in case what you order for isn't what you get. You should also ensure that you check their customers' reviews to know how good their results are. Some hatcheries usually would require that your purchase a particular number of chicks, and most times, it's a minimum of twenty-five. This technique is for their body heat to be retained.

If you however desire to get your fowls personally, you could go to a local farm, pet store, or the farmers' market. Most of these places would be stocked with all sorts of chickens, especially around the Easter period. Once you get to these places though, ensure that you check how they care for their fowls. The drinking water must not be dirty or clogged up with fecal droppings. You should also check to see if any dead birds are lying around.

- **How to spot a healthy chicken?**

This by far comes as a very crucial point. When buying your chickens, what are the very things to look out for? How can you tell a healthy chicken apart from a sick one? How do you know those that are injured or weak? Follow the tips below:

- Check the eyes of the fowl: The first thing that characterizes a healthy fowl is the eye. A chicken with unclear, or drowsy eyes. No matter how beautiful a chick looks, a drowsy eye is one big indicator of sickness. Also, a chick that has the skin around its eye red and swollen is bad for business. The chick should also not be blinking too much.
- Check the foot of the fowl: Do not buy chickens that have issues with their feet! If the feet are spread widely apart, bent, or with turned-in toes, you might have issues later on with them. Another thing is that most chickens are susceptible to having a foot disease even at their early ages. So, them scaling through or not depends on their health status. So, if the one you want to get already has that issue, it could mean it's not too healthy. The scales on the leg of a chicken should also be smooth with flat plates.
- Watch the chick's behavior: Chicks are always up and bustling with their combs as red as blood. If you see any chick pecking dangerously at the other, avoid it!

- Feather: What you want is a chick with smooth, flat, soft, and dry feathers. Seeing spots of skin with no hair could be an indicator of the presence of lice or mites.
- The beak: The beak protuberances of the fowl should be even. None of it should be broken.
- Physique: You want to get a bird that can stand without limping or falling over. The chick should be able to stand tall without drooping.
- Check the nostrils of the fowl: An unhealthy chick will have discharge lining its nostrils.
- Listen to the sounds the fowl gives off: Wheezes, sneezes, coughs, or rattles should not be heard from the chick.

- **Preparations to be made before buying your chickens**

Yes, you are excited about owning your chicks, but do you know that they'd need some warm place to stay in? You will also need a lot of supplies to get started. You don't want to start setting up their house after you must have made your purchase. A few of the fowls could die in the process. For older chickens, ensure that the house you are using for them is safe! You don't want to see holes that rats or skunks could make their way through. You'd also need to have a drinking trough, feeding trough, grit, and chicken feed available. If you are raising layer birds, the best cage to work with is the battery-cage system. You could also work with a building with concrete floors. Just ensure that the litter you need—wood shavings—is already set.

For chicks, you might need to go the extra mile. First, they'd need a lot of light and warmth, so ensure that is supplied. You could get a brooder box for this purpose though. Some sources of heat include the following:

- Incandescent bulb
- Heat lamp
- Bulbs.

You will also need feeding troughs of small sizes and water troughs. To help young chicks digest their food well, you might want to add a little bit of sand to their meal. These sand particles go down to the gizzard where their food is crushed into tiny bits. If you are using an open-mouthed drinker, you might also want to add stones to the water in it to prevent the birds from falling in it, and then, drowning.

## Chapter 3

## Housing Your Chickens

Housing your chickens will help the birds stay safe and protected as they would be free from predators, and the consistent scorching of the sun. Doesn't sound convincing enough? Let's look at a few more reasons why you should indeed spend much in getting the right shelter for your chickens.

1. Not everyone is fond of chickens. Chickens that do not have a house could easily wander off to some other house, and stir trouble. If you do not want trouble with your neighbors, get a house for them.
2. Getting your chickens a proper house will help them live longer and happier.
3. To keep your chickens warm during the night, you should get them a secured shelter where they can stay when the sun sets.
4. Chickens are very fond of passing out fecal matter consistently. And most times, the droppings can be very hard to remove from your

backyard. So, to solve this problem, you should just get a cage whose floors are covered with litter that will absorb the droppings.
5. Hens also desire warm places to lay their eggs, so getting a house for them would make things easier. Besides, if you let them lay in someplace in your yard, it may take a lot for you to find them. Hens don't want their eggs to be easily found by predators, so they do a great job in hiding them.

**Chicken Housing Options**

There are several choices to make, but then, the final decision lies in you knowing what is perfect for them. Several factors determine what house they get, and they include the following;

- The number of chickens you plan on raising
- The size of your backyard.

What housing choices are then available?

**Free-Range Housing**

This type of housing will allow your chickens to go anywhere they want within an open but confined space.

## Advantages

1. The chickens slay eggs that are healthier than the ones laid by the confined fowls.
2. The fowls get to mix without any restraint.
3. You will not have to provide food for them since they'd take to eating natural food substances like weeds, grasses, tiny grains, and insects. This technique would no doubt help you save money.
4. This technique will protect your fowls from lice and mites.
5. These fowls will feed on the bugs that prey on your plants.

## Disadvantages

1. Predators could easily prey on them since they would potentially be exposed to them. The only

thing that could guarantee their safety is if they have a wall that surrounds where they stay.
2. Free-range chickens might be wilder than the domesticated ones.
3. If you are free-ranging in your vegetable garden, these fowls could mess up your tomato fruits and also feed on all the leaves in there.
4. The fowls raised with this style will hardly roost or make use of the nesting box.

This style is good for farmers with numerous birds. Also, if there is no possibility of a predator harming your fowl, then, there's no issue at all. Try the free-ranging system. All breeds of chicken would do well in a free-range system, except for the Cornish Cross. Those enjoy being fed in isolation. Here are a few tips to make you enjoy raising your chicks.

- The predators mentioned above will not attack your fowls once they see you around.
- Do not fix a regular time to visit your chickens. The predators could notice that and choose a different time to strike their attacks.
- While you are with your chickens, you could frighten the predators by making obvious sounds.

## Cages

You could also try housing your chickens in cages stacked in spaces like your garage. You could choose to suspend these cages from tree limbs or get them fastened to the walls of your house or fence. These cages are usually constructed with strong wire strings that are connected in the form of a mesh. There are different sizes to which a cage could be built, and it all depends on the number of chickens that you want to raise. For this kind of housing, you can work with either a wired floor or a solid floor. A wire floor will require that you place some container beneath the cage that the fowl's droppings would land in, while a solid floor would require you to use liter or any other bedding materials.

Choose cages that are resistant to adverse weather conditions. This technique will prevent you from spending on the same utilities and supplies twice. Most of the things you should be getting should be constructed from logs of timber that are thick enough to resist damages caused by rain, snow, hail, and even sun rays.

## Advantages

1. This style will help ensure that your chickens are ready to be bred.
2. If you are raising your chickens for the aim of shows and performances, this system is inarguably the best option as they'd learn to be confined to cages.
3. Chickens get more comfort and support when they are on solid floors.
4. This kind of cage would give you no issue when cleaning.
5. Your birds would have no issue with ventilation since the structure practically has holes all over it.

## Disadvantages

1. This wire used in constructing this kind of housing could prick the toes of the birds if the cage isn't constructed using the right dimensions.

2. This cage will place a restraint on the movement of your birds, consequently leading to some disorders with their metabolic functions.

So, if you have a limited space to keep your chickens, you could try out this method. Also, as a beginner, if you plan on starting small, you could adopt this method. One thing you should however take note of is the fact that this kind of cage exists outdoors, so, you might need to construct an outdoor shed. The best breeds for cages are the Bantam chickens. They are small enough to live comfortably in them.

When building a cage, you could employ the following tips;

- The size of the holes of the floor should not be too wide, otherwise, the toenails of the chickens could get stuck within the wire netting. In the process of them trying to escape, they might end up injuring their toes. So, to prevent such occurrences, it would be better to just go for solid floors. If you are raising breeds like bantams or broilers, that idea is just the best.
- When it is time to clean the cage of your poultry birds, you could easily let the birds out first. This

way, the fowls even get to stretch their limbs from time to time. All you just need to do is fence the area so that they are not preyed upon by predators.

## Shelter and a Run

This system of farming, just like the name implies is a large cage that your fowls can run to in case of adverse weather conditions or when they need to lay their head somewhere. So, it's like a combination of the features of a free-range system and a cage. Here, you should ensure that the area where they free-range is protected from predators.

## Advantages

1. This technique is great for you if you aren't too sure of the predators in your yards. You could keep them in the cage when you are not around

them, and let them out when you can keep your eyes on them.
2. This kind of cage usually is hardly covered, so, your fowls get a lot of sunshine and fresh air.
3. If the shelter or cage is high enough, you'd get the privilege of walking in to feed the chickens. It would also be easy to gather the eggs laid by your hens too.
4. This system could be very beneficial if you have some vegetable garden you don't want your fowls tampering with.

**Disadvantages**

1. You will need a lot of space or yard to construct this kind of cage.
2. This kind of cage might require you to invest in a lot of capital.

So, the shelter and run cage system is the one you should go for if you plan on starting small at first, and then, expanding gradually later.

## Chicken Tractor

This tractor is a cage with wheels attached to its bottom. You could place this kind of cage at any place in your yard. A standard chicken tractor has about two or four wheels. The wheels just make it convenient to move the cage from one place to the other. So, when one side gets sunny, you could move the cage to somewhere cool. Chicken tractors are usually constructed using several dimensions, all depending on the number of fowls you want to raise.

With wooden pillars held together by wire strings, and a special compartment that your chickens can lay their eggs, you've got the perfect chicken tractor. This tractor usually houses the basic supplies like feeding troughs, drinking troughs, and roosts. However, there's usually no floor as the fowls are in direct contact with the grass in your garden. The chicken tractor is more of an enclosure that traps the fowls within a spot. Also, you wouldn't have to worry about predators with this style.

**Advantages**

1. Sometimes, your fowls need more than the minerals and nutrients offered by the processed feeds and grains. This technique of housing chickens allows your birds the freedom of feeding on insects, roots, and some other natural grains that they like. These things supply them with Calcium and other minerals that they wouldn't get somewhere else. It would also help if you are laying layers, as they'd be able to lay eggs with tougher shells.
2. The mobility of this cage will allow you the grace to move the cage to warm spots during cold seasons like winter. And also, during the summer, you'd get to move the cage to cool regions.
3. Since your birds' droppings land directly on the grass in your garden, they get naturally fertilized. So, you should move the tractor through all the

squares of your vegetable garden to get the whole thing fertilized.

4. Moving the cage around your garden will make your fowls feed on all the insects and parasitic bugs in your garden.
5. The fresh air your fowls enjoy here will make them less susceptible to catching diseases.
6. Constructing this cage might not require a lot of capital as you could easily make use of recycled supplies like plastic pipes, and wooden crates. You might even get to build it without spending a dime if you have all the necessary items.
7. With this system, there's little or no maintenance that needs to be done. Most time, what makes poultry stressful is the cleaning of chicken litter. However, here, they pass their droppings directly on the grass. Also, since the cage can be moved, the droppings don't have to accumulate in one place.
8. Also, if you decide to clean out a portion of soil that your fowls occupied before, you don't have to let the chickens out of the cage. You could just push them to another corner of the garden while you clean up the place.

## Disadvantages

1. The chicken tractor is not as firm and stable as a real cage that just stays in a place. Usually, it is affected by adverse weather conditions like wind, sun, or snow. This kind of cage also might not be able to protect your birds from water or air.
2. The fact that this cage is not all too sturdy means that a big predator could easily push it off its stand. This point becomes very consequential if you are living close to the forest.
3. The fact that water can easily get into this cage means that the fowls' feed could easily get moldy.
4. During a condition like winter or intense rainfall, the garden will not be a nice place to keep the fowls. So, you might have to move them to an enclosed and warm area. If you don't have an enclosed place like this, this might not be the right option.

So, the chicken tractor is what you need if you have a large garden, and little time to spare for maintaining a cage. If you also live in a place with a low incidence of predators, you might also want to try constructing this kind of house. To make this system work out better, you should always ensure that you shift the cage to other areas of your garden. You should also ensure that you do not put the cage in areas that are susceptible to flooding. You could instead position the cage on grounds of higher slopes. Lastly, during the cold seasons, keep your fowls inside some warm and enclosed space.

**Buy or Build a Chicken House?**

This is the area where we get to talk about carpentry skills, and that is because regardless of whatever option you choose, you will still need a bit of touch added to it. Several places offer already built chicken houses, and if you want, you could choose to build them yourself. Now, let's look at a few things that could help you decide what option to choose.

1. You should start by getting the total cost of either of the options; The cost that is being referred to here covers the price of the option and other things like transportation. The price of most of the finished cages usually differs depending on the intricacy and fanciness of the cage. Even with this option, you'll still need to set up the house in your yard. If you don't want to do that by

yourself, you might want to consider the price employing someone would attract. However, if you don't want ready-made houses, you could gather information about the price of the supplies you'd be needing. This option gets even more costly if you don't have any of the tools. So, you might have to get every single one of them, right from the saws to the hammers and even to the nails. If you don't mind that factor, you could search for ideas on the internet to see what others have done with their creativity.

2. You have to make a choice that you can work with—i.e., something very easy to construct and affordable. When searching for ideas on the internet, ensure that you take note of the money you are willing to invest in a cage. You don't want to get something that won't leave you extra money to feed your chickens. For ideas, you'd find out that most of them are free, but the more exquisite ones might require that you view them at a price. You could get some DIY ideas here though—https://morningchores.com/geodesic-dome/

Another thing you should consider is the number of fowls that you want to keep within the cage. The more the fowls, the more expensive the cage you want to construct might be. Lastly, you will need to decide where the cage would be fixed in your yard. Sunny areas are usually the most ideal options.

**Building a Proper Chicken House**

1. First, you will need a nesting box, and that is used for cleaning the litters of the box, and for gathering the eggs laid by your hens.
2. A large door that leads to the cage will help you to be able to easily access the cage and your chickens. It would also make it easy for you to change their feed or water.
3. There has to be a latch through which you could pass some securing lock through to avoid a situation where someone invades in.
4. Wire strings around the cage will help to keep the predators away, as they would not be able to reach your birds. It would also allow air to be able to breeze in freely through the coop. You

could also close up all the openings with a piece of hardware cloth.
5. A floor that is proofed to avoid attacks by predators: Rats and squirrels are always attracted to chicken droppings, and so, they'd want to find their way into the cage. But then, you can avoid the issue by building a short fence around the cage.
6. Simple cages can be completed with nails, screws, and sheets of corrugated steel.
7. You could leave a bit of space beneath your cage to make it easy for you to collect the chicken droppings.

**Basics of an Ideal Chicken Coop**

The basic things you should take note of when building a chicken coop include the following;

**Size of the Coop**

You always have to remember the fact that chickens do not like being enclosed in places. The more chickens you are raising, the bigger the cage has to be. It would also be good if you constructed something big at first, as you might want to increase the size of your flock as time goes on. You have to ensure that the building is tall enough that it doesn't get buried by snow when it's snowing. There should also be a space allocation for nest boxes, drinking troughs, feeding troughs, and dust baths.

## Location of the Coop

When deciding where you want your cage to be located, you might need to consider the following options.

- How accessible is the cage? You have to ensure that despite the condition of the weather, that you can access your chickens. You must also be able to clean up the cage without going through any hassle?
- Shade: You have to ensure that the cage is fixed in a place with shade so that it does not get hot during the summer. If the cage you build is directly beneath the sun, the fowls could end up growing uncomfortable.
- Sun: During the cold seasons, your fowls would want to feel a lot of warmth. So, you could position the cage so that it faces the south. The windows should face the east and west. In case you build some overhead covering for your birds

during summer, you could take it off during the winter.
- Drainage: You do not want a situation where your poultry's floors are muddy and wet. That could potentially increase the number of pests and parasites, and that is detrimental to the health of your fowls. Besides the pests, the chickens would get dirty and smelly, once they attempt to lay on the muddy ground. To solve this issue, you can place things like old rubber tires, or some other solid stump within the cage so that the birds can stay out of the mud.

## Insulation of the Coop

Insulating a chicken coop will help keep your fowls warm during adverse weather conditions, and also help to prevent the buildup of moisture and humidity within the coop. So, using objects like Styrofoam to insulate the coop will go a long way to help.

## Cross-Ventilation

There has to be a way that air can easily breeze in and out of your chicken's cage. The best thing you can do is to ensure that your fowls' cage is built in such a way that the windows are directly opposite each other. At least, the cage or coop must have about two windows. When these birds pass out fecal droppings, it releases ammonia that could cause them series of issues with their respiratory tracts. You could try fixing vents to the roof of the coop too to allow for proper ventilation of the cage. This style will help to prevent the accumulation of dangerous gases, dust, or heat within the cage.

## Storage Space

The cage should have a place or room attached to it where you can store the unneeded supplies like the feeding troughs, and drinkers. You could also make use of your garage space for this purpose, as the supplies wouldn't be stained with the dirt from moisture and temperature.

## Nesting Boxes

Your chickens have to have a place where they can easily lay their eggs. That's where the importance of these boxes comes to play. Having your chickens laying on the bare ground could get the surfaces dirty, and sometimes, the birds could even break it with their activities. Ensure that you have about one of these boxes for three hens, at least. Also, ensure that you place the nesting box in a place with plenty of light. To prevent a situation where the fowls take the nesting box's roof as a sleeping spot, ensure that it is constructed in a sloppy style. Lastly, you could build the sides of the boxes up a bit to prevent the eggs from rolling out.

## Flooring

You need to find something that would easily absorb the droppings of your fowls. Examples of these litter materials include wood shavings or dirt. A wooden floor can easily take in the moisture that's in the air, and also, promote infestation by mites. To avoid the wood from getting destroyed by mites, you might need to fix a sheet of vinyl across the floor. A floor made of concrete is usually the best option since it is easy to clean once you lay the right adsorbent litter on it. Then, it is not the type of floor to get destroyed by predators, termites, or moisture.

## Electricity

During the cold seasons, you might need electric bulbs to offer warmth to your fowls. Also, you could heat water for your birds during the cold seasons with electricity wired into the poultry. At least, with that style, you would not have to go back into your house to fetch water. Having at least one or two light bulbs brightening up the cage will also help your hens to lay even at night. Also, when things are foggy outside, the bulbs could be sources of artificial light.

## Temperature

Chickens also get affected by high temperatures. So, once the temperature of the environment increases to something in the range of 95- and 100-degree Fahrenheit, they'd become temporarily inactive or cold. Chickens can also suffer from conditions like frostbites, so, you need to consider providing heat for your chickens.

## Access to Feed and Water

You have to ensure that the feeding and water troughs are placed at a distance that is comfortable for your fowls. If you decide to hang the troughs from a height, ensure that it is one that they could easily crane their necks to drink from. Also, the bottom of the troughs should be at the same height as the bird's upper back. Using this technique will ensure that their feed and water do not get messy.

## Roost

The roost should be placed above the nesting boxes to ensure the hens do not spend the night in the nesting boxes. Sticks that are wooden rounded with their edges sanded or flat wooden planks can be used to build the roost. The roost's lowest bar should not be more than 18 inches from the ground level; this is to ensure that heavy breeds can get to it. Likewise, the bar of each roost should be well spaced to ensure the birds do not poop on each other and also to help prevent the bullying of chickens from their bullies.

Lastly, the width of the roosting bars should not go below 2 inches for a full-sized chicken.

**Droppings Board**

Your chickens are bound to poop, which is why a droppings board placed beneath the roost will help you to collect chicken poop easily without it spilling on the bedding. You can then remove the droppings each morning, putting them in a bowl and discarding them in a compost. This action helps to lower the ammonia present in the atmosphere, thus keeping your chickens healthy. For your droppings, you can use a fixed or removable droppings board built from a large wooden plank.

**Runs and Yards for Your Chickens**

Fowls are one of those birds that love running around to feed on insects. So, even if you want to build them an enclosed cage where they are to stay all day, you'd still have to make provisions for a yard. Sometimes, you might need to clean their cages, and let them out too, so, ensure that you fence the yard to protect them from predators such as hawks or possums. You could also choose any of the following depending on your chicken farming goals.

**Confined Runs**

If you want to have runs that don't smile at predators, you could work with materials like hardware clothes. Use the material to wrap around the runs and the window openings of the coop. To fix the material to the windows, make use of screws and nails. Also, to stop animals—predators from digging their way to the bottom of the cage, you can pile about twenty-five inches of hardware cloth along the pathways for the run. For areas with bears, and other wild animals, you could line your fences with electric barbs.

**Dust Bath**

This bath will prevent pests and ticks from sticking to the bodies of your fowls. Most times, these pests stay in the feathers and the legs of birds. So, it's advisable to have baths where they can rub their bodies in. The bath is usually in the form of a box that is filled with sand or some other gritty substance that would rub against their skin. Having a dust box for your chickens will be best appreciated during the cold seasons when your chickens cannot rub in the outside.

## Cleaning the Chicken Coop

This issue is indeed an issue because chickens always poo every single time. An accumulation of these droppings can cause their litter to become messy and smelly. The smell usually attracts predators like rats, so you have to ensure that you change it as soon as possible. The first thing you can do about that is to change the litter or bedding as frequently as possible. Also, an unclean coop will make your fowls look dirty and unwelcoming. You should utilize bedding materials like pine shavings, and sawdust. Materials like hay aren't too much of litter materials, so, ensure that you don't make use of them. You could also make use of biodegradable bedding, as it can later pass for very good compost material.

To clean your chicken coop, you'd need the following supplies; buckets, wheelbarrows, rubber gloves, and face masks.

## Protecting Your Chickens From Predators

Several predators could prey on your fowls, and here, we will look at a few of them. We will also see how they can be held back from carrying out their attacks. First, you need to know that predators are one of the big issues that poultry owners face, even from the small poultry owners to the large farm owners. Second, let's look at some of these predators.

1. **Raccoons:** This predator is one of the deadliest that could ever prey on your fowls. Once they gain entry, you might not even have a single chicken left. They are very smart and no matter how much resistance they face, they'd most likely still get what they want. They are so deadly that they could reduce an 8- or 10-gauge wire to nothing. So, no matter how strong your fowl is, a raccoon would gladly reduce it to nothing.

   To avoid them from gaining entry into your poultry, ensure that you add wire strings to your chicken cage. Then, you can go ahead to connect these strings to a firm piece of wood. Also, when constructing your cage, you have to ensure that there are no free cavities through which the raccoons can burrow through. If after this you are unable to stop the raccoons from getting into your cage, you might have to resolve to use traps to eradicate them. And that's because once these raccoons find out that there's food somewhere, they might never want to leave.

2. **Foxes:** This predator makes free-ranging very difficult. Foxes love chickens and would do anything or go to any lengths to get them. They could even burrow into the ground if it means getting their hands on them. Foxes are very smart creatures, and so, it might require you a lot to get their eyes off your fowls.

One thing you could do to avoid this issue is to get a guard dog that would effectively keep the foxes at a reasonable distance from your fowls. Although, this option might not be the best if you have a small flock of chickens. Another thing you could do is to ensure that the grass in your garden is cut short so that the foxes won't be able to creep up on the chickens sneakily. You should also ensure that there's nothing else that could blend any approaching fox with your environment.

Escape boxes will help to keep chickens out of the reach of foxes, so, you could place them around your garden. Electric fences are also another great ways through which foxes can be kept away from your chickens. A perimeter skirt is another way through which you could avoid foxes. This skirt is a fence that's about six inches tall. Then, it's usually bent towards the outer edges by six inches. So, the moment any predator tries to burrow through the bottom of the coop, their further access would be prevented by the perimeter skirts.

3. **Coyotes:** Coyotes are the very lovers of chicken. Something note-worthy needs to be discussed about this predator though. When efforts were made to thin the population of coyotes, it was discovered that the opposite of what was needed was done. Why? You killing the other coyotes will effectively reduce the competition between the several ones that were initially there. And that means the ones that weren't killed would get more food to themselves. From here, they'd reproduce, and then, the number of coyotes would increase.

However, there is a good side to these predators though. Once you have coyotes in your garden that aren't giving you issues, it'd be better if you let them be. They are territorial animals that would usually mark out their regions, and this technique of theirs will help to chase away the other bad coyotes. However, if the ones you have in your garden are the destructive ones, you might need to reach out to the Wildlife Agency. The board usually would offer the best options.

4. **Hawks, eagles, and owls:** These present more issues to the table than the other predators, and that is because one could not possibly eradicate all of them. There'd always be more. Also, these animals are protected by laws like the Migratory Bird Treaty Act of 1918. Going against that law means that one would pay a fee of about two hundred and fifty thousand dollars.

   Even with these laws, there are some other ways with which one could prevent the, from preying on your poultry animals. Most of the hawks out there are usually on the watch out for chicks that are not guarded by their mothers. These hawks would first observe the chickens from a safe and proximal distance—usually trees— before heading over to deal with the chickens. So, you could start your prevention by ensuring that there are no high spots or old trees in your garden. All you need to ensure is that there's no place where they could fix their feet when they find your chickens. Another thing that could keep the chickens away is by fixing shelters in your garden that the chickens can use as a shade. Once they are out of sight, the hawks would leave.

Owls prowl about at night, so, all you need to do is to keep your chickens in some safe place that they wouldn't have access to. Also, ensure that whatever material you use for caging your birds in is made of tough material. This technique will ensure that the birds can't break through the net and then, find their way in.

You need to know that the major way to stop predation is by stopping the animal from becoming a problem. Once an animal becomes a predator, you might need to go through several lengths to alter its behavior. In case you've tried methods like fencing and the use of exclusion devices, and there's little to no change, you shouldn't give up. The other way you could avoid the pests listed above is by contacting your state's wildlife agency to know the predator management laws that govern your place. Some states allow landowners to offer themselves any form of protection from wild animals. So, they get the right to end the animal's life in the process, even.

Lastly, ensure that you aren't the one causing yourself trouble with predators. Most of them are usually attracted to the chicken's feed, so, you need to ensure that you don't give your chickens more than what they need. The extra grains would in no doubt bring the raccoons to close.

**Chicken Mortality Management**

This topic has to do with all that is involved in the management of a chicken's death. Why do chickens die? Honestly, there are several reasons—sickness, dominance, too much mating, and so many other similar reasons. Sometimes, when a chicken looks frail and close to the gates of death, we are faced with either of these four options, as regards what we can do with the chicken;

- Deciding on whether or not to rescue the fowl.
- Killing the chicken humanely.

- Thinking of how to properly dispose of the corpse.
- Thinking of what is to be done after the death of a chicken.

**Do you wish to rescue the chicken or not?**

You need to realize that the business of poultry is filled with times where the birds die. But sometimes, by rescuing your chickens, you could prevent deaths by a long extent. If your chicken gets sick and fails to bounce back within three days, there's a high possibility it dies if you don't intensify the care, you mete out on it. With this method, you might get lucky enough to not kill your bird.

The first thing you can do as a beginner is to reach out to other chicken owners around you. It helps when these people have a particular level of expertise though. They'd be able to recognize the chicken's disease from the symptoms its displays, and then, you can give it the right medication. To make this step active, it would be right if you called them in earlier though, so that if you have to purchase some extra medication, you'd still have time on your hands.

You could also go ahead to reach out to a veterinarian doctor who would come over, look at your chicken, and then, offer the right sets of medications. Sometimes, the vet doctor could offer your fowl with injections that go right to the bloodstream of the bird. Even with this method, if the sickness has eaten too deeply into the fowl's body, the fowl may end up dying. So, in all, you have to ensure that you monitor your chickens closely so that you can easily notice them when they are down.

**Killing the chicken**

If you wish to end the life of a chicken, it'd only be humane to do it quickly and neatly. Do not try any technique that will only prolong the chicken's sorrow. You can start by pulling the neck of the chicken slightly to the left or the right, depending on which of your hands that you work more with. Then, you could go ahead to run the sharp edge of a knife along the length of the neck. If you are not skilled with this thing, ensure that you get an expert that will show you how to kill a chicken.

Mostly, all you need to do is pull at the neck and twist it slightly at the same time. This technique is to dislocate her neck bones, and if you use the knife quickly, the whole thing would end in no time. Most of the sick birds do not usually offer a lot of resistance, so, it's usually easier with them. Once you are done, check the bird to see if you can find any sign of life in it. You could pull the neck again to be sure of that. A dead chicken is usually still and unmoving.

**How to handle the remains of a chicken**

Once the sick chicken is dead, you are now saddled with the responsibility of getting it disposed of. Since chickens are domestic animals, you do not need any sort of approval from the government. Now, let's look at a few things you should do to dispose of the remains of a chicken?

- Bury it under a mound of soil.
- Burn the remains.
- Have the body bagged and then, you could put that in the bin.
- Hand it over to a vet doctor for disposal.

The following points are the things you shouldn't do to dispose of your chicken;

- Do not cook it! It was sick, and you did not know what went wrong with it.

- Do not use the remains as composting material. It only works if you have a system that can digest foods such as uncooked chicken strips.
- Do not feed it to carnivores' animals. They could get the same sickness too, you know? Besides, doing that could give the animals a strange liking for chickens, and maybe the very predators for your other chickens.

When burying a dead chicken, it is advisable to first place it in some cardboard box. Although, it's not a must you follow that technique though. Also, to ensure that other animals don't smell it and then, dig out the ground again, ensure that you make a hole about 50cm deep before doing the actual burying. To make things better, you could even go as far as to place a rock over the spot.

**What is to be done after the death of a chicken?**

Death always comes as one shocking and saddening event, and it might hot you more if you have a small flock. The pain gets even more grievous if the said chicken is the fattest of the lot. However, farmers shouldn't get bent over the death too much. There are several questions you have to consider as soon as possible to avoid more deaths.

- Do you plan on continuing with the poultry business?
- What caused the illness in the last bird?
- How can you possibly prevent the sickness from befalling the others?
- What other adaptive measures could you possibly take?
- In case there's another breakout like the one that caused the death of your chicken, do you have the necessary medication on ground for emergencies?

Knowing the answers to the questions above will go a long way in preparing you for the future.

## A Short message from the Author:

Hey, I hope you are enjoying the book? I would love to hear your thoughts!

Many readers do not know how hard reviews are to come by and how much they help an author.

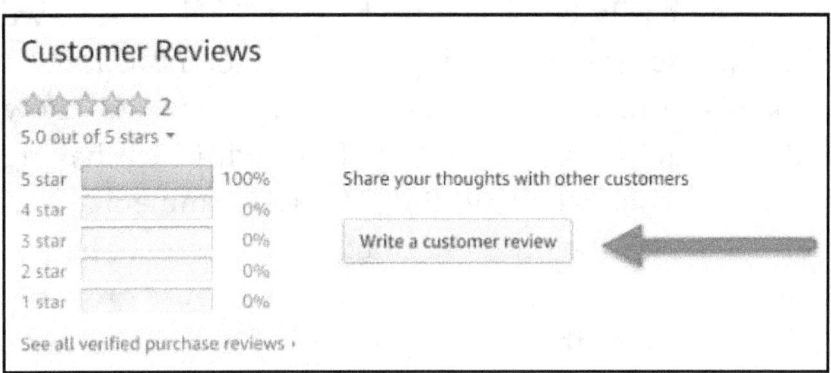

I would be incredibly grateful if you could take just 60 seconds to write a short review on Amazon, even if it is a few sentences!

>> Click here to leave a quick review

Thanks for the time taken to share your thoughts!

# Chapter 4

# Feeding Your Chickens

Just like humans, chickens need food to survive and grow. The food a chicken eats is usually referred to as feed. It comes in form of grains, granules, or powders, which can easily be picked up by their beaks. Here, we will take a look at everything you need to know about a chicken's feed. First, as a beginner, you need to know that there are different kinds of feed, with each having different proportions of the necessary minerals and ingredients for the different categories of birds. There is a kind of feed for chicks, one for those that are growing, and for the ones that are in their old ages. For example, the growing birds might need a lot of calcium for strong bones, while the older ones need some other mineral. So, these different feeds have different concentration levels that are all aimed towards seeing your birds grow healthily.

## Chicken Feed Types

There are different types of feed, and they all come in textures so different that your chickens can easily pick up with their beak.

1. **Pellets**: This kind of chicken feed is usually in form of very tiny balls. So, in a whole bag of feed, you have millions of those balls that your chickens can eat. This type of feed is very good because your chickens would be able to easily pick them up from their feeding troughs. Even if your chickens get too active and then, knock their feeder over, you could easily pick the pellets back up, inadvertently avoiding wastage. Pellets are also easy to pour for your chickens, and they don't get affected by too many factors.
2. **Mash:** This is a powdery form of chicken feed that is mostly fed upon by chicks. The reason this kind of feed is the best for chicks is that they'd be able to easily digest it, and then, grow. There are several kinds of mash feed that chickens feed on, and you could even add a few bowls of water to the feed to get that marshy texture that almost all the chickens love!
3. **Crumble:** This kind of feed is somewhere between the mash type of feed and the pellets. It's just that it has a texture rougher than that of the mash feed. It is also not as compact as the pellet feed. Most times, this feed is used to shift the

focus of a fowl from mash to pellets, i.e., like a sort of gradual introduction. This feed can be fed upon by any class of poultry birds.

4. **Shell grit:** The reason your fowls need this grit is for the digestion of their food to get faster. The grit usually would find its way to the gizzard of the fowl, and then, help in grinding the food particles. This way, they'd be able to access the nutrients available in the feed better. This grit also helps to boost the calcium levels of a fowl, especially the laying ones. Calcium is one major mineral that improves the strength of eggshells. If you are practicing the free-range style, you might not need to worry about feeding your chickens with this though. They always find grits on their own, so that's okay. However, for those working with the cage systems, you will have to provide them with this, except that you do it in a separate container. Your chickens know instinctively the quantity that they need to feed on.

5. **Chicken scratch:** Most times, this feed type is mistaken for actual chicken feed. However, it is a mixture of chopped corn and other essential grains that help to supplement your chicken's

diet. This feed type will supply your chickens with tons of energy, and that will consequently help them stay warm on cold nights. To prevent your birds from gaining too much weight, do not feed them with too much of this feed!

6. **Medicated and un-medicated feed:** Most of the chicken feed out there usually comes in either medicated or un-medicated varieties. The medicated kind of feed contains Amprolium that helps to prevent diseases like coccidiosis. However, if your chickens have previously been given doses of coccidiosis vaccines, you need not use the medicated feed. The ingredients employed in the feed are usually not friendly with the ones in the vaccine!

7. **Fermented feed:** This refers to the feed that is already mixed with water. Then, you allow it to ferment naturally. The process of fermentation usually lets the majority of the nutrients in the feed come active. With this kind of feed, you won't also have to spend much since the increased thickness would make your birds feel fuller.

## Feed for Chicks

The feed for chicks comes in two types; there's the grower and the starter feed. The latter is usually fed upon by the newly hatched chickens, and they feed on it until they are about six weeks of age. The starter feed is usually packed with a lot of essential proteins (about twenty-five percent) and is designed to fulfill all of their needs as chicks. When they fall into the age range of 6 to 20 weeks, you can now start feeding them with the former. The grower feed contains fewer proteins and more Calcium, which is necessary for the development of bones. Too many proteins fed upon by growing chickens could cause them to suffer from issues like kidney or liver problems as they grow.

## Feed for Egg-Laying Hens

This feed is packed with minerals that help to meet the needs of laying hens, and they include proteins, calcium, and some other essential vitamins. All of these vitamins and minerals usually work to increase the quality of the laid eggs, as well as increase how frequently the eggs are produced. This feed contains about 16-18 percent of protein, and a huge allocation is taken by the calcium constituent. This kind of feed should be fed upon by chickens that fall within the range of twenty weeks of age, or after they have started laying.

You could also get the normal feed for chickens, and then, supplement it with calcium sources like oyster shells or the crushed eggshells of fowls. Apart from a feed rich in calcium, your laying birds would also profit from fresh fruits and vegetables such as;

1. Bok choy
2. Silverbeet
3. Endive
4. Cucumbers
5. Melon
6. Squash
7. Strawberries
8. Broccoli
9. Lake
10. Vegetable peels
11. Cabbage
12. Fruit peels, etc.

## Feed for Meat Chickens

There are different kinds of feed produced for meat-feeding chickens, and they include the starter, the grower, and the finisher. For chickens like broilers, that have short life-spans, you could feed them with feed that is densely packed with proteins, as it would encourage them to grow very fast. Ensure that you are not feeding the feed for broilers to the laying hens, as it could cause series of complications. The finisher feed is the one that most broilers are fed with.

**Foods to Avoid**
1. **Fatty foods:** Foods like flock blocks and sunflower seeds are very rich in fat, and may contribute to the Fatty Liver Hemorrhagic syndrome that will end the life of your fowls suddenly. You need to realize that the fact they feed on usually would form around the liver, consequently making it soft and susceptible to bleeding. Most of the fowls that suffer from such syndromes are usually overweight ones.
2. **Too much salt:** Several chickens have suffered from salt poisoning, and that is because salt is not necessarily a part of a chicken's diet. So, you have to ensure that whatever you are feeding your chickens with isn't packed with too much salt.
3. **Nightshade plants:** Examples of these plants include potatoes, tomatoes, eggplants, and

rhubarb leaves that contain toxic compounds like oxalic acid, and solanine. However, if you plan on cooking them before feeding your chickens, you'd have succeeded in breaking down most of the toxic compounds and that is okay.

4. **Onions:** You have to ensure that you are not feeding your chickens with too many onions, as it contains thiosulphate which contributes immensely to the destruction of red blood cells that cause anemia or worse still, jaundice. And in birds, that can be a pretty serious issue.

5. **Avocados:** This fruit contains a toxic substance known as persin that causes the necrosis of the myocardium in chickens. And that issue usually leads to the heart-stopping in its actions.

6. **Apple seeds:** This fruit contains cyanide that can be pretty much detrimental to your chickens. If you are going to feed your chickens with an apple, ensure that the seeds have been plucked out first.

7. **Citrus fruit:** This food substance usually causes a drop in the production of eggs.

8. **Dried and raw beans:** This particular food contains hemagglutinin that is highly dangerous to chickens.
9. **Chocolate:** This one contains methylxanthine which is also dangerous to chickens.
10. **Moldy food:** Ensure that you do not feed your chickens with bad bread or overripe fruits on which mold has begun to appear.
11. **Garden plants:** Several garden plants are pretty harmful to your chickens, and they include the following;
    - Belladonna
    - Bloodroot
    - Bull nettle
    - Bracken
    - Byrony
    - Careless weed
    - Castor bean
    - Cocklebur
    - Curly dock
    - Delphinium
    - Fern
    - Foxglove
    - Ground Ivy

- Hemlock tree
- Horseradish
- Holly
- Ivy
- Lantana
- Lily of the Valley
- Lupine
- Periwinkle
- John's Wort
- Tulip
- Yew

**How Much Do I Feed?**

The amount of feed that is needed by fowls mostly depends on the number of fowls that you have in your flocks. The more chickens you have, the more chicken feed you will need. Also, if the kind of chickens that you are raising tend to be the very active ones, you might need a bit more or less than ¾ cup of chicken feed per day. Now, how many times do you need to feed your chickens? First, you need to consider how many times you'd be available for this. If you are the kind that goes out in the morning and gets back at night, you might need to feed them in the morning and the night.

Another thing you need to take note of when feeding your chickens is that over-feeding could attract birds, squirrels, rats, and some other pests to your fowls' cage. Free-range chickens don't usually eat too much though, since they'd find food substances in some other place. Always ensure that you don't give your chickens less food than they need.

Broilers for example feed on more feed than other birds. Most times, they are always found feeding for the first two to three weeks. After three weeks, you might need to give them unlimited feed for the twelve hours that follow. You should also ensure that you do not feed your chickens with too many teats as they would end up eating less of their actual and much-needed feed. Even if you have to feed your chickens with treats, ensure that it is less than 10% of their actual diet.

**Chicken Feeders and Waterers**

**Chicken Feeders**

Chickens, thankfully are not too picky when it comes to choosing how they feed. Most times, they wouldn't care less if you scattered their feed all over the ground. They'd just eat it, and even make a mess of it. This is where the importance of feeding troughs plays out. This way, the feed is not made a mess, and it remains just as clean as you want it to be. It will also prevent their feed from littering the whole feeding area; so, you would not have to fight with predators like rats. Remember rats are vectors of diseases, and if you aren't careful enough, they could get transferred to your flock.

Now, even while discussing feeders, we need to note that there indeed is an ideal type that will do the best job at keeping your chicken's feed clean. Let's take a closer look at the good things such feeders are capable of doing.

- Your chickens can have a constant feed supply all day long as they have extra sloppy compartments where you can stack the feed in. This technique will no doubt ensure that your chickens lay all day round as they have a regular food supply. Some feeding troughs don't have this feature, so you have to check for an opening at the top to be sure.

- The right feeding trough will ensure that your fowls don't waste food, and that can help to keep the pests away. Once that happens, you wouldn't have to consider the money spent on chicken feed.
- The trough is easy to set up. Most feeding troughs need little to no set-up before you can start using them, while some other sophisticated ones need.
- It is easy to clean. Getting a feeding trough with compartments that can easily be pulled apart for cleaning is one of the things you should be on the lookout for.
- It is resistant to water.
- It can be gotten at a moderate price.
- The feeder allows several chickens to feed at the same time. This one particularly depends on the size of your flock. The more chickens you have, the wider the trough must be.

## Plastic or Metallic Feeding Trough?

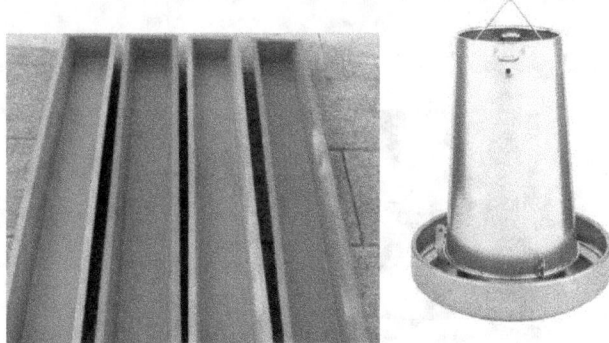

Feeding troughs crafted out of metal will undoubtedly last longer than the ones crafted from plastic. However, the metallic troughs are becoming very rare to find as it could be pretty hard to find metal scraps. Plastic on the other hand is cheaper to produce and is what most of the manufacturers want to work with. It is also easy to clean, and might even last a long time if you handle it with care and subject it to only a little pressure. Plastic will break during the winter seasons, and might even end up getting bleached if you leave them out in the sun.

Some of the metallic feeders work on the self-feeding principle, as the chicken might have to stand on some platform, and then, push a lid that covers the feed aside. This way, the feed can get protected from rats and other wrong factors like humidity. This kind of feeder is called the treadle feeder.

**Hanging Feeders**

This method is by far one of the best ways of offering food to your chickens. There's usually a handle attached to it through which a rope is strung. It is this rope that is then tied to some support in the ceiling. To make the feed available for chickens with this method, you could just trickle a bit of it down the opening at the top of the feeding trough. If you are using this kind of technique, you might want to get several feeding troughs so that all the chickens can have access to the feed you are supplying to them. If that is not done, there could be the issue of congestion, and dominance by the stronger fowls.

**The Trough-Styled Feeders**

With this kind of feeder, several hens could feed at the same time without hassle. However, you should ensure that the kind of trough you get is the one with props attached to it. Since it is an open-mouthed feeder, the props would help to keep mud and other dust particles from settling into the feed. This kind of feeder will also not allow the chickens to sit down on them or poop on them. And that is because its structure does not allow for that to happen.

## Chick Feeders

These kinds of feeders are smaller than the adult-sized ones, and so, they have the appearance of troughs with rounded bottoms.

**Determining the number of feeders that your flock needs.**

The solution to this issue lies in you being able to determine how much volume of storage you need. For six hens, you might need to provide them with about a quarter volume of feed each day. So, you might need a large feeder to contain that much feed. However, in all, you should ensure that you don't get a feeder that can hold up too much feed. The following are the reasons for that;

1. Too much feed means that your chickens would spend more time trying to finish it. And during that time, the feed could get damp and moldy.
2. If you peradventure forget the trough outside because of its heavyweight, you'd end up having a lot of mice and raccoons attracted to your chickens' cage.
3. A big feeder might eat up too much space in the cage, and that might not be too feasible if you have several chickens in your cage. So, you might have to consider how much space you can do away with.
4. When there's too much food in the trough, there's a big possibility that the chickens end up wasting a large amount of it.

**Chicken Waterers**

This is also known as water troughs. Their importance cannot be better emphasized, as, without them, your chickens could die if they are in an enclosed space. There are different kinds of watering troughs available, and they include the following;

- Gravity Waterers
- Nipples Waterers

- Chicken cups

Now, before you choose any kind of waterer, you have to ensure that you consider some things first. Here, we will look at three key things that would help to determine the kind of watering trough that you need.

1. The number of chickens in your flock
2. The kind of breed you are raising
3. Do all your chickens live in one coop?

First, you need to know that one waterer is usually prepared for about six chickens. If your flock comprises smaller chickens who could easily cower away from the drinking trough when a bigger chicken comes to face, you might have to get about two or three drinking troughs. It all depends on the amount of space you have available for the extra troughs.

Secondly, there are some breeds of chicken like broilers who cannot do without drinking water intermittently. With those kinds, you might have to get as many drinking troughs as possible. Well, it's either that or you get ones that are big enough to take as much water as possible. Another thing to consider under this section is the fact that your chickens will drink more water on hot days than they would do on hot days, and this reason boils down to the theory of homeostasis. So, if your chickens drink about two pints of water on a normal day, you should increase it to two on a hotter day. Breeds like bantams usually would drink less than other breeds of chicken though.

Thirdly, you have to ensure you have one water trough per coop.

**Types of Poultry Waterers**

There are several kinds of watering troughs, and already we listed them above. Now, we will go into explicit details as regards what they are and how we could make the best use of them.

1. **The chicken nipple watering trough:** This kind of water trough will keep the water clean for long hours. The chicken nipple waterer might just need that you change the water once every week. However, in hotter climate situations, you might need to change the water more often. This watering trough is a five-gallon compartment that can keep your chickens hydrated for several days. All you just need to ensure is that your chickens are good with nipple waterers. Not all chickens

can adapt to this style of drinking, and that's where the issue usually lies.

2. **Traditional gravity fill watering trough:** This is the type of watering trough that you will see in most poultry farms. It is structured in form of a bell that is turned upside down. It is usually suspended from a chain and will offer water to your chickens conveniently. This kind of watering trough is available in different sizes and can be constructed from either plastic or metal. Most importantly, they are easy to use, and they work best even for small flocks.

3. **The chicken cup watering trough:** This kind of trough is almost the same as the chicken nipple waterer, except for the fact that the nipples are replaced by drinking cups. So, if your chickens are finding it hard to adapt to the use of nipples, you might want to work with this kind instead. The only issue with this one is that the water in the trough can easily get contaminated with dirt. This kind of trough can cover about ten chickens or more.

# Chapter 5

# Breeding Your Chickens

Breeding refers to the processes involved in the hatching of eggs and the raising of chicks. Hatching of eggs can be done both naturally by a hen, and artificially by stacking them within incubators. And the eggs becoming actual chickens depends on whether or not the eggs have been fertilized by some rooster. So, in this section, we will look closely at the process of breeding chickens.

First, let's take a look at a few reasons that should make you want to breed chickens;

1. Egg production
2. Meat production
3. Private consumption
4. Competition and shows
5. For passing away leisure hours

For the purpose of this book, we will focus on egg and meat production.

What are the advantages of breeding your chickens though?

1. If you breed your chickens, you might not have to make any expense getting new ones.
2. It could be very nice to watch your chicks grow into big chickens that yield lots of value. It makes you feel like you have lived every part of their lives with them.
3. You might not even need to breed them as long as you have hens that can help you follow through with the process through natural means.

So, let's jump right into the process of breeding chickens

**Implement a Breeding Plan**

This stage settles on the various things that you need to do before you start to breed your chickens. There are questions that you need to first ask yourself. For example,

- Why exactly do you want to breed your chickens?
- Do you think you would have enough time to spare for the intensive care they'd need?
- If you aren't breeding them the artificial way, do you feel sure that your hens can help with that?

The answers to the questions above will help you know what plan to choose. The plans will subsequently be discussed as we go further.

**Breeding Methods**

The two common ways of breeding chickens include the following;

1. The flock breeding
2. The Pedigree breeding.

**Flock breeding:** This type of breeding usually will give your chickens the opportunity of breeding alongside other hens. Here, there's usually only one male, and that makes everything pretty much easy.

**Pedigree breeding:** This is the type of breeding that is done when you want your chickens to exhibit certain traits. For that to happen, you could start by mating the cock that displays the said qualities with another equally good hen.

**Breeding Chickens For Egg Production**

This section is for you if you desire to sell the eggs your chickens lay. The production of eggs by a female would usually slow down after the hens lay for some time. So, to prevent a situation where you have to purchase new hens every three years, you could breed yours too. But one thing you must implement to get the best result is the principle of cross-breeding. Most of the fowls of the supposed pure breeds have been groomed mostly for shows, and so, cannot lay efficiently again. Ensure that you breed the eggs from the very good layers in your flock, as these traits would be transferred to the chicks.

## What to Feed Your Breeder Chickens

The kind of feed that you feed your chickens would no doubt help to promote the fertility of your cocks and hens. For more fertilized eggs, you might want to start feeding your chickens with feed rich in protein. You might also need to add calcium food sources to your chicken's feed to ensure that the eggs are strong. Lastly, feed rich in protein will help with the fertility and hatchability of the eggs.

## What to Feed Your Broody Hens

A broody hen is more like a moody hen. During this time, she will not feed on much feed. She might also not leave her laying spot for some days. Even if she does, it might just be because she wants to eat, or drink water. Immediately she is done, she'd head back to her eggs and continue to brood over them. Because of how less frequently a broody hen eats, they should be fed with the feed of starters.

**Supplements**

Supplements are important, but you have to ensure that you don't feed your chickens with too much of them. However, when a chicken is brooding, you might need to supply it with these things so that they'd feel a bit energized, at least. Some of these supplements include;

- Vitamin A: The moment a chicken stops feeding well, it is prone to suffering from the deficiency of this Vitamin. One thing you'd notice instantly is the fact that the lack of this Vitamin would cause your fowls to grow in a stunted manner. There are also several other symptoms like dry eyes and a decreased resistance to infections. To fight this, you could feed the broody hen with vitamin A-rich foods like kale.
- Vitamin D: When a chicken is deficient in this vitamin, you will instantly notice a decrease in egg production. So, you have to always ensure that your hen doesn't lack this particular vitamin. Other issues could arise as a result of its deficiency and those things include eggs with

thin shells. To avoid this issue, ensure that your chickens stay beneath the sun for about thirty minutes. You could also add cracked eggshells to their meal, or better still, oyster shells.
- Vitamin E: The deficiency of this vitamin can be solved by feeding your chickens whole grains and fresh greens.

## Incubation of Eggs

This is a term that refers to the artificial hatching of eggs. So, for this, you will not need hens or any other female hens to brood your eggs for you. All you mostly need to ensure for a successful incubation is that you have fertilized eggs. Most times, incubation is only recommended to be taken up by those who have large flocks of chickens. And that is because hens may not be able to brood too many eggs. And also, the artificial incubation of eggs is usually faster than the natural method.

Another thing you need to take note of is the fact that incubation will require a lot of fuel, energy, and time. So, you shouldn't have one for yourself except you are a big-time farmer that has thousands of hens. For sole proprietors that want to still incubate their eggs artificially, you could just hook up with hatcheries that will help you to hatch your eggs at minimal prices.

**Egg Selection**

This step is one of the things you need to put into consideration when artificially incubating your eggs. It will help you know what eggs you ought to stack into your incubator and what eggs you ought not to. One thing that people do to select the right eggs is called candling. This is the process of studying the innermost parts of an egg with the aid of very bright light rays called candling devices. The word, 'candling' was culled from the word, 'candle' as a candle was the first source of light that was used for this process.

You could also use the candling technique to determine how old an egg is, and whether or not it is fertilized. Now, how can you tell? Once you direct a light ray towards the center of an egg and barely see the dark yolk, then, you can say that you've got a fresh egg. However, if you notice a dark spot at the center of any other spot, that means that the egg is bad. You could easily tell that an egg is old once you begin to see the yolk moving about the egg without any hindrance. Yolks are supposed to have a relative degree of thickness, and stability.

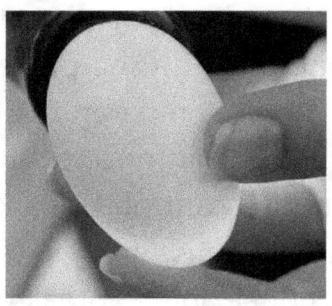

To candle your eggs, all you need to do is hold them with your thumb and first two fingers. Then, use your other hand to direct the flashlight to the larger side of the egg. To access the sides, tilt the egg to any angle you want. You could candle your eggs for the first fifteen days of incubation, but after the sixteenth day, ensure that you don't do that anymore! At that time, the eggs in your incubator must not be shifted at all. And even if you do, you might not notice much as the chicks would have begun to develop over that time.

**Temperature and Humidity Control**

Before you use an incubator, you must check the temperature ranges that are available for those models. Most of these incubators usually differ in the temperature and humidity that they offer, and that's true because most of them are forced-air incubators and some others, fresh-air incubators. The forced air incubators should work at a temperature of $99.5^0F$ and the still-air incubators should work at temperatures like $102^0F$. As you continue with the process of incubation, you'd notice the certain temperatures that work best to incubate your eggs. Humidity control is usually not as crucial as temperature control, but then, both of them need to be tuned to effective points. If that is not done, the chickens may not be able to break out of their shells. They may even end up suffering something as disastrous as omphalitis at their tender ages. Omphalitis is a situation where there's a difficulty in the absorption of a chick's yolk sac, and that could lead to infections by bacteria or death once the chick is hatched. In some other cases, the chicken may die two weeks after they are hatched.

Several incubators have humidity devices attached to them that help to provide the eggs with the needed moisture. Some of these devices may need to be filled manually, while the others have devices that are tied to the incubator to intermittently provide the eggs with moisture. To control the humidity yourself, you could just make use of the vents attached to it. Opening the vents will reduce the humidity while closing it will increase it. What most hatcheries want to have is a humidity figure of 60%. To be very accurate about the humidity of your incubator, you might need to purchase a hygrometer.

**Cleaning Your Incubator**

You have to ensure that you clean out your incubator after you finish hatching a set of eggs. Refusing to do this crucial task could cause a progressive decline in the rate at which your eggs are hatched. Why? The dirt usually would transfer bacteria and diseases to the eggs very quickly. Most times, the risk of infection comes when a single incubator does the work of incubating and hatching. To solve this issue, it'd be best if you purchase two or more incubators, with some allocated for incubation, and the others for hatching.

While cleaning, you also wouldn't want to use chemicals on any part of the incubator. These chemicals too contribute immensely to the reduction in the success of future hatches. The best cleaning media is warm water with very mild bleach. Then, you could scrub the corners with brushes. After cleaning, you'd need to ensure that you leave it to dry before putting it to use again.

**Hatching Chicks**

**Chick Hatching Process**

How do you know when your chick is about to hatch out of the egg? Once you notice a pip in the egg, you could term it as ready. A pip is a small hole that a chick makes in an egg when it's about to break out.

Once the pip appears, the chick follows within twenty-four hours. In some cases, though, there could be a few exceptions like the size of the egg, the temperature, and the humidity of the hatchery. Sometimes, you could find a couple of unhatched eggs and some other ones that would just not hatch. However, before you discard them, ensure that you run a candling test on them to know the ones that they contain.

## What To Do With Your Hatched Chicks

Once your chicks are hatched, the first thing you want to do is to feed them with the starter feed that was discussed earlier in this book. At this stage, you might not be able to readily differentiate the female chicks from the make chicks, so, separating feed for layers and growers would not be necessary. If you got your eggs hatched naturally, the first thing you might want to do is separate the broody hen from her chicks for the first few weeks. You can start to introduce the chicks to the rest of your flock once they are old enough. If you notice any issue, you could separate the chicks from the older ones again.

However, with incubators, after your chicks get hatched, the first thing you want to do is take them to a brooder that will make their feathers dry and soft. Moving them about while they have wet bodies will make them die almost immediately. To make a brooder, get an enclosed area, a heat lamp, and a food tray for the chicks. You could use the shavings of pine wood as the bedding. Also, ensure that they get enough fresh air as possible. At first, it's advised that you keep the temperature of the incubator as high as possible. Then, as time goes on, you could decrease it to lower ranges. After that, they'd be good to go without the brooder.

**Potential Chick Hatching Issues**

Most of the issues that most chicks face have much to do with the wrong temperature or humidity setting. However, you can avoid most of them by having the right plans, and procedures. One issue is that of your chicks having crooked toes. It usually occurs when the temperature in the incubator is too low. The other common issue is that of splayed legs. And that occurs when the incubation tray is too smooth. So, once the chicks hatch, and can't get a proper footing, they could come out with splayed feet. So, ensure you stay away from incubators with smooth trays when purchasing an incubator.

## Keeping Records

Keeping records will help you know where if your incubator is good enough or not. So, all you need to do is to keep a record of the chickens that hatch, and the ones that do not. This way, you can work on your mistakes as the year progresses. The best way by which you could keep your records is by marking your chicks. Some things that you should take in a note while keeping your records include the following;

- The color and gender of the chick.
- When did you start the hatching process?
- When did you end the hatching process?
- How many of the chicks hatched out of their shells?
- How many of the chicks did not hatch from their shells?
- What was the average temperature and humidity that you worked with?

## Likely Chicken Breeding Issues

Here, we will take a look at a few diseases that young chicks can contract during the first few weeks of their lives.

1. Coccidiosis: This disease is one of the commonest causes of diarrhea in chicks. It usually occurs when your chicks eat the droppings that they find in their feed or water. The best thing you can do to fight this issue is by ensuring that their brooder is clean. You should also ensure that you get rid of any dropping you see in the feeding and drinking troughs every time you want to refill them.
2. Hunger: Once a chick does not get fed two days after it has been hatched, it might end up dying. The moment a chick is hatched, it'd usually get most of its food supply from the egg yolk. Another issue that could cause them to starve is if you place the feeder too high for their beaks to reach. If your chicks aren't eating on the first day, you could encourage them to do so by filling a small box with a little bit of food. That way, they wouldn't have to eat the litter.
3. Feather or toe picking: Most chickens usually end up pecking at something, and if they find nothing worthy of that, they may end up pecking at their toes or feathers. This attitude that they display is pure because they still can't tell the difference

between actual feed and other things that don't feed. Also, as feathers begin to grow out of their body, they could get curious about what the things are, and then, start pecking at them. So, to discourage this bad habit, you really should provide your chickens with as much feed and water that they can lay their beaks on. Also, ensure that the feed you provide them is highly rich in protein.

4. Sticky bottom: The droppings of chicks are usually sticky, soft, and messy. And if you don't take care of that, it could harden and clog their anal openings. And that could inevitably lead to their death! If it gets hardened though, you could dab the end of a towel in warm water, and then, use it to dab the opening with the hardened poop. You could try doing that very gently to avoid tearing their skin open. Once it gets dry, you could proceed to use some antibiotics to clean the spot to prevent a reoccurrence. To avoid this issue, you have to ensure that your chickens are drinking as much water as possible.

5. Splayed legs and crooked toes: These two issues occur mostly during incubation. Most times, once

you move these chicks to brood sites, the issues can be avoided. What causes this issue is the slippery plate of an incubator. The best way of correcting this issue is by tying their legs together with a thin string of thread. This technique could take a few days or weeks even for a correction to occur. So, to avoid this issue generally, ensure that your incubator and brooder are set to the right conditions.

## Caring For Newborn Chicks

1. Chicks are just like newborn babies that need a lot of tendering and love. So, you have to ensure that they have to themselves all that they need—feed, water, and light (warmth). As for the feed, you have to ensure that you go for the starter feed! However, most of these preparatory steps should be done before the chicks arrive. You have to have arranged everything within the brooder—feeding trough, drinking trough, and the light sources. The brooder has to be big enough to give each chick a space of about three to four square feet.

2. The source of the light should either be a light bulb or something else that can expel enough heat for your chickens to feel warm. The source of light should be about three feet above the chicks though. You may need to reduce the heat after some time though. As for the bedding of the brooder, you could work with wood shavings. Always ensure that you get rid of the wet litter to prevent the build-up of pests and diseases. The odor could also affect the chicks too.
3. For the first twenty-two hours of the week, ensure that you provide them with light consistently. A 40-W light bulb is usually enough for the chicks. The feeders have to be about four inches apart from each other though. Lastly, as for the water troughs, you could feel watering troughs about a quarter way up. You have to see that you introduce chicks to water as soon as possible. The water usually helps to keep the chicks hydrated. You might also want to add a bit of glucose to the water to give your poultry birds strength.

**Proper Handling of Eggs**

Handling your chicken's eggs the right way will help you to ensure that the eggs are of high quality. Now, let's look at a few general things that you need to consider when handling your eggs.

- Layer house Management: The quality of the egg that you get from your poultry house is related directly to how well you take care of your chickens. Likewise, feeding your chickens with feed rich in calcium like oyster shells, water, and minerals are amongst the several things that can affect the quality of your eggs.
- Coop and management of the nest: Ensure that you keep all your laying chickens in fenced areas so that you can have ideas as to where they lay their eggs. Sometimes, when some people practicing the free-range kind of farming eventually find the eggs laid by their hens, they'd have already gotten old. Sometimes, you might not even locate the eggs.
- Clean environment: Ensure that you keep the places where your chickens stay clean and dry. When eggs are laid in muddy sites, they become

dirty or stained too, and that can make them get infected by strange strains of bacteria. So, ensure that you deeply clean their nest boxes every two weeks.
- Ensure that you clean up the wet litter in your chicken coop, and also ensure that there's a good drainage system.
- Ensure that you provide a minimum of four nesting boxes for your chickens. This technique will help to minimize the rate at which the eggs get cracked. You should also ensure that the nesting boxes are stashed with enough litter that will help to reduce breakage.
- Ensure that you visit your poultry as regularly as possible so that you can easily gather the eggs laid by your hens. To do this, you might need to note the time that they lay their eggs in the day, so, that you can always make it in time. The longer you keep an egg in the nesting box, the more likely it is to get dirty, or broken. Ensure that you at least visit your poultry two times a day. You also should get used to picking up eggs laid by your chickens to avoid dirty habits like eating eggs and the likes.

- Ensure that you keep animals like cats and rats away from your coops as they could either eat the eggs or infect the nesting box with diseases.

**Egg Cleaning and Handling**

Here, a few guidelines are discussed on how you can clean and handle your eggs.

1. Ensure that you gather your eggs in containers that you can easily clean. Examples of such include plastic containers and egg flats. All these things will help you to prevent issues like rust stains, and contaminations. These kinds of things are usually hard to disinfect.
2. Ensure that you do not pile up too many crates of eggs. At least, if you are working with the plastic trays, ensure that you don't use more than five of them. This technique will go a long way in preventing breakage.
3. Ensure that you cool your eggs before cleaning them. The eggshell would usually tighten up its pores and push out the dirt particles once they are cooled.
4. As soon as you pick the eggs from the nesting boxes, wash them. This technique will help to

prevent contamination or reduction in the egg's quality.

5. When washing your egg, ensure that you use water at a temperature of $99^0F$. This technique will make the eggs perspire, and eventually, that would push the dirt out of the pores. While doing this though, ensure that your eggs don't sit in water. Once the water cools down, they could easily take in the contaminants present in the water.

6. Immediately after washing your eggs, ensure that you dry them immediately. When you want to stack them in the crates, ensure that you do that with the large side up. Once you keep your fertile eggs at a temperature that's above $85^0F$, you can be sure that the germinal disc would develop in no time.

**Grading and Sorting Eggs**

You need to grade and arrange your eggs before you sell, store or eat them. The best way by which you can access an egg is by using the candling method that was described earlier. Using this technique will help you to get rid of cracked eggs or the ones with strange matter inside them. Examples of this strange matter include blood spots.

It's also necessary for you to pick out the cracked eggs. Once you notice a fine and sometimes slight white line on the surface of your chicken's shell, know that it is cracked. And the moment you apply a little bit of pressure on them, they could end up breaking open. You could either get rid of the cracked eggs, cook them, or give them to your dogs.

You could also grade an egg using factors like the depth of the egg's air cell, the outline of the yolk, and the albumen. The air cell depth of an egg is the distance between the top of the egg and the bottom of the egg when you tilt the side with the air cell upwards. The air cell depth in fresh eggs is usually less than one-eighth of the egg's length. The older the egg gets, the bigger the air cell gets.

The yolk is another determining factor. The one of a fresh egg is usually surrounded by a thick layer of egg white. This egg white is commonly referred to as the albumen. So, once you shake the egg, it moves a little bit away from the egg's center. Already, the subject of the yolk has been discussed. The egg white in a fresh egg usually would not shift when the egg is rolled. That is because a fresh egg has a thick egg white.

## Spots

Once you notice an egg with spots of blood or flesh that is more than 1/8 inches cannot be eaten. However, you should take note that there is something in an egg called the chalaza that resembles a line of tissue. It helps to hold the egg yolk in place within the albumen, so, that's fine.

**The other issues you could find in an egg include the following;**

- The wrong shape of an egg
- The wrong egg texture, etc.

## Storage of Eggs

When you want to store your eggs, you should take note of the following points.

1. Store your eggs in paper or plastic egg crates with the small side down to keep the air cell fixed in one place.
2. Ensure that you mark dates on your egg cartons so that you can discard the older eggs first before

moving on to the newer ones. In all, ensure that your eggs are discarded within the first five days that you pick them up from the nesting box.
3. You should store your eggs at a temperature between forty and forty-five degrees. Then, also at a percentage humidity of seventy percent.
4. Ensure that you do not store your eggs with materials that have distinct smells like fishes, onions, and tomatoes.
5. Ensure that you never keep your eggs above room temperature or at low humidity. Doing this would certainly cause the eggs' quality to reduce.

## Requirements When Selling Eggs

There are no regulations that bind the sale of eggs when you are raising less than three thousand layers. But the moment you have more than three thousand hens, you might need to attend to a few other things.

For a flock that is less than three thousand layers;

- Ensure that you sell the eggs within five days.
- Ensure that you refrigerate them at a temperature of $45^0$F or less.

- Ensure that you do not work with cartons meant for other businesses to sell your eggs.
- Each of the cartons that you use should have the following details inscribed on them;
    - The name and address of your poultry.
    - The date which you packaged the eggs
    - The statement of recognition for the eggs.
    - The average number of eggs in the crate.
    - The 'Keep Refrigerated' instruction.

It would also be great if you could size your eggs. The sizes are usually denoted in ounces per dozen.

- For small eggs, you have a size of 18oz.
- For medium-sized eggs, you have a size of 21oz.
- For large-sized eggs, you have a size of 24oz.
- For X-large eggs, you have a size of 27oz.
- For jumbo eggs, you have a size of 30oz.

## Cooking and Handling Egg Foods

You always need to let your consumers know that they need to refrigerate their eggs until they are ready to use them. You should also ensure that you don't store your eggs with food substances like onions, or fish that have a pungent odor. If you are going to make use of pasteurized eggs, use them for things like egg nogs that do not need the eggs to be cooked e.g., eggnogs, and ice cream. Lastly, when making something with eggs, ensure that you do not leave them for more than twenty minutes after you have cracked them open.

## The end... almost!

Hey! We've made it to the final chapter of this book, and I hope you've enjoyed it so far.

If you have not done so yet, I would be incredibly thankful if you could take just a minute to leave a quick review on Amazon

Reviews are not easy to come by, and as an independent author with a little marketing budget, I rely on you, my readers, to leave a short review on Amazon.

Even if it is just a sentence or two!

So if you really enjoyed this book, please...

>> Click here to leave a brief review on Amazon.

I truly appreciate your effort to leave your review, as it truly makes a huge difference.

## Chapter 6

## Raising, and Butchering Meat Chickens

If you are raising your chickens for eating meat, then, you will at one point or the other have to kill them. In more professional terms, it is regarded as butchering. The reason you should try raising your chickens is that you'd have the grace to monitor what they feed on, and indirectly, protect your health or that of whoever is eating it. Most of the other things involved in raising chickens have already been discussed in this book.

There are several ways with which you could raise your chickens intended for meat and they include;

- Obtaining the meat quickly and cheaply by working with breeds like the Cornish Cross chicks. Then, grow them using finisher feeds that are highly rich in protein. In the end, your chicken has the taste of the one sold at the mall.
- Raising your chickens the normal way but with a little bit of the conventional methods. This point involves you feeding your confined

chickens with finisher feeds, but still allowing them the chance to feed on grasses and other matter outside.

The chicken that is used for the majority of commercial purposes is the Cornish Rock hybrid. They are usually fed every twenty-four hours of the day. However, as opposed to the thoughts of most people, they weren't injected with growth hormones. Their fast growth was primarily because of their genes, and nothing else. Most people however do not accept commercial chickens because of the seemingly jam-packed way they are raised, and how they are jointly killed. Sometimes also, their meat was reported to have tasted inferior to the other well-bred chickens.

**Raising Meat Chickens**

**Selecting The Right Chickens**

When you are choosing chickens to butcher, you have to consider their breeds. Some breeds grow so fast that you'd get a lot of meat from them, while the rest are so lean that they'd be better raised for their eggs. Some of the breeds of chicken good for meat include the Cornish-White Rock Hybrid, Plymouth Rock, Orpingtons, and Wyandottes. You might also want to consider the gender of the chicken. Occasionally, males are usually better, bigger, and more delectable than females.

- Capons: These are castrated male chickens, and that technique will help to ensure that the male grows faster than normal since their energy won't be channeled to meat production. For this stage, White Rocks and other breeds of chicken work best.
- Cornish Game Hens: This is the chicken you get when you order for a gourmet. It is usually soft, and tasty, even though it is a female.

## Selecting The Best Time To Raise Chickens

You can raise chickens at any time of the year, but then, if you are thinking of selling them, you might want to adjust your raising time to one that is close to the festive seasons. The climatic condition of where you live is also another thing to consider. Most times, people slaughter meat during the cold temperatures when only a few flies are moving about.

## Number of Chickens to Raise

As a beginner, you might not want to exceed twenty chicks. Well, the number usually would depend on the number your family can consume. For example, if you eat a chicken per week, then, you might need fifty-two chickens for the whole year. However, you shouldn't raise that many at the same time as you might have to spend a lot of money on feed and the chicks themselves. Also, if anything goes wrong—maybe an outspread of disease, all your chickens could die.

You also need to consider the fact that chickens raised for eating don't have long lifespans. So, if you are not going to sell them or give them out as gifts, you might need to raise a few. You wouldn't want them all getting ready to be killed at once. One more thing that you need to consider is the fact that raising many chickens at once will require you to have a big freezer, a large coop, and tons of money.

Consider the following when raising chickens for meat;

- Give your chickens good feed, and also ensure that their litter is dry.
- Ensure that your chickens live at the right temperature.
- Have a feeding routine, and stick religiously to it.
- Ensure that you keep predators out of the coops.

## Butchering Your Meat Chickens

The butchering time is that period where you kill your chickens for their meat. And here are a few things to put in mind about this step.

- Breeds like broilers are not meant to live long. They have a short lifespan.
- You might need to properly plan the day by getting the right set of equipment ready.
- If you have any relative that is emotionally attached to the chicken, you might need to keep them away.

## Are Your Chickens Ready?

You can eat your chickens at any stage of their lives, but then, if you could be patient enough, you might get the fattest bone. For breeds like broilers, once you feed them with the right finishing feed, they'd be ready for consumption within eight weeks. Other breeds like the Cornish-rock hybrid might take longer before they are ready for consumption. You should also take note of the fact that an old chicken would have tougher flesh than a young one.

## Get a Butcher or Do It Yourself

If you feel that you are emotionally stable and skilled enough to go through with this, then, you should. But then, sometimes, getting a skilled person to do the job means a faster job, and less of a mess. To butcher your chickens yourself, ensure you;

- Get a place to butcher your chickens.
- Get a lot of water to wash off the blood and other nasty stains.
- Get a place you can dispose the residue.
- Have lots of time!

## Killing The Chicken

Before you get to this stage, it is assumed that you have all the necessary equipment. So, you can start right away with the killing process. You should do this early in the morning so that you'd be able to get the chicken you want while it's still sleeping. Or you could get the chicken the night before, and have it bound in someplace. Now, what are the options that you should not even try?

- Electrocuting the fowl.
- Using a poisonous gas.
- Shooting the fowl.

- Drowning the fowl.
- Using power tools to rip the head off.

However, you could kill the bird neatly by following the steps below;

- Grab the chicken by its hind legs and then, hold it with its head pointing downwards until it stops quivering.
- Use your other hand to grab the ax you'll use for butchering. The chicken should still be held upside down.
- Hastily fix the chicken's head to the stump while ensuring that the head is held between the nails you previously planted.
- Use one hand to slightly tug at the legs, and at the same time, stretch the neck out.
- Use your other hand to cut across the neck quickly.

If you use a knife, ensure that you cut from the top of the neck to the back. Stop at a point just below the head. Your knife has to be sharp enough, and your hand steady. You also shouldn't stab the chicken's neck. Rather, run the knife slowly across the neck in a slicing manner. As for shears, you could use heavy pruning shears.

Other killing techniques include;

1. Killing the bird with a stick: To do this, place a thick stick on the ground. Then, place the neck of the chicken beneath it. Then, you could place a foot on one end of the stick while ensuring that you pull the chicken's feet upwards with a firm grip. This technique will break the chicken's neck.
2. Wringing the neck: Start by leaving the chicken to dangle with its head down. Grip the neck firmly, and then, twist it sharply around. Sometimes, this would result in you pulling the head off the neck.

After killing the chicken, the next thing to do is to remove the feathers. You can do this by immersing the whole chicken in hot boiling water. After that, you move on to scalding it. If the water you used earlier isn't hot enough, this might get pretty difficult. Once the water gets cluttered with feathers and blood, change it. Before you begin to get rid of the feathers, ensure that you wear gloves to protect your hands.

The next thing to do is to check out the flesh before you. Is it as fat as you thought it would be? While doing this, you could check the birds for signs of diseases. A healthy fowl will have either white or yellow skin. Things like blisters could mean that the chicken was roughly handled. Here are a few things that you should watch out for;

- Abscesses: These are lumps that occur either outside or inside the fowl's body. These lumps are usually filled with pus, and that's unhealthy.
- Tumors occur anywhere in the body. Some may be soft and the others, hard.
- White or pale livers with white spots all over it.
- Sores on the body of the chicken.
- A butchered fowl that wasn't attended to for more than one hour at a temperature of 40ºF.

To remove the neck, ensure that you gently get rid of the crop, gullet, and tracheal passageway first. To do this, cut beneath the neck, and end near the body. There, you'd see two tubes. If the crop is filled with food, you'd instantly notice a small bulge. Don't squeeze it too much as it could get the meat contaminated once the contents spill out. The trachea is usually rigid and with folds. So, to cut the crop off from the neck, follow the lines of the gullet. Once you cut it down to the shoulder part, you can now cut off the crop.

The oil gland is usually the bright yellow spot at the hind part of the tail or the bottom of the spine. When you need to get rid of the organs, follow the procedures below;

- Place the body on a table with its rear end facing you.
- Rip the skin and the flesh apart with your two hands moving in opposite directions.
- Push your whole hand through the hole you've formed, and then, curl your hands once they get in. This move is to pull the organs to the rear end.
- If you like, you could keep the heart, liver, and gizzard. The gizzard should be split open though to get rid of strange gritty objects. There's also a yellow lining that you'd need to get rid of.

**Meat Collection, Cleaning, and Storage**

This is the last stage of the butchering process. After you must have washed the cut pieces of meat, you have to bring the temperature of the body to something as low as 40°F. Once you can work them to this temperature, you can then begin to pack them up for storage. Follow the steps here to end on a good note.

- Rinse your meat pieces with a solution of bleach and water; ratio three to one. Then, you can use hot soapy water.
- Run the insides with cool running water. Ensure that you check for feathers and the leftover organs.
- Place the body on some surface and then, pat it dry with a paper towel.
- Wash the kidneys, liver, and gizzards well before storing them.
- Cutting your meat into small sizes will make it easy for you to store them in the freezer. For that, you'll need a very sharp knife. However, if you plan on roasting the whole body of the chicken for a barbecue, all you need to remove is the neck and the head.
- If you are packaging the parts to sell them, you might want to consider cutting up the breasts aside and placing them in a separate pack.
- When cutting, move your knife through joints rather than across bones.

- You could use plastic freezer bags to pack your chicken until you are ready to freeze them.
- Before freezing your chickens, ensure that you have enough space in your fridge first.
- Ensure that you chill your meat to about 40-degree Fahrenheit or lower for freezing.
- Do not stuff your meat into the fridge until you have checked the maximum pounds that the fridge can support. Trying to freeze more could mean that a long time has to be reached before the whole thing gets frozen up. That extra time is enough time for bacteria to grow all over it.

# Conclusion

Chickens are very lovely herds that are fun to raise and yet, offer so much—meat, eggs, and more. As a beginner, you should ensure that you take note of every precaution discussed in the pages of this book as they would go a long way to help you raise healthy and happy chickens. If you are raising your chickens for their eggs, ensure that you give them feed that is highly rich in calcium. For meat-offering birds, feed your birds with a lot of feed rich in protein. You should also bear in mind that there are different kinds of feed for different kinds of chickens. To avoid your chickens getting sick, change the litter often, give them the right vitamins and medications, and pay much attention to them as possible. With the information encapsulated in this book, you are on your way to building a successful chicken farming business in no time.

I wish you the very best.

# References

Parwati, P. (2020, May 16). *Top 10 Most Popular Chicken Breeds For Beginners*. HOBI TERNAK. https://hobiternak.com/most-popular-chicken-breeds/

Farm, R. (2021b, March 15). *Choosing a Chicken Breed: How to Choose the Right Chicken*. ROYS FARM. https://www.roysfarm.com/choosing-a-chicken-breed/

Singer, F. H. (2020, August 29). *How to Buy Your First Chickens*. Homestead Survival Site.

https://homesteadsurvivalsite.com/how-to-buy-chickens/

Staff, M. (2018, December 20). *Housing Your Chickens: All You Need to Know to Do It Properly*. MorningChores. https://morningchores.com/chicken-housing/#:%7E:text=On%20average,%20a%20minimum%20of,get%20buried%20in%20the%20snow.

Bradford, E. (2019, December 13). *30 Geodesic Dome Ideas for Greenhouse, Chicken Coops, Escape Pods, and More*. MorningChores. https://morningchores.com/geodesic-dome/

Market, H. A. (2021, January 21). *How To Prevent And Manage Common Backyard Chicken Predators* ». Heritage Acres Market LLC. https://www.heritageacresmarket.com/chicken-predators/

A. (2019a, November 15). *What to Feed Your Chickens, and What Not to Feed Them*. Freedom Ranger Blog. https://www.freedomrangerhatchery.com/blog/what-to-feed-your-chickens-and-what-not-to-feed-them/

Coop, T. H. C. (2020, December 14). *Poultry Waterer: Which Is Best For Your Flock?* The Happy Chicken Coop. https://www.thehappychickencoop.com/poultry-waterer/

Hm4, L. (2021, March 7). *How to Breed Chickens | Ultimate Guide*. Mile Four. https://milefour.com/blogs/learn/how-to-breed-chickens#17

Clauer, P. (2021, May 2). *Proper Handling of Eggs: From Hen to Consumption*. Penn State Extension.

https://extension.psu.edu/proper-handling-of-eggs-from-hen-to-consumption

www.ingramcontent.com/pod-product-compliance
Lightning Source LLC
Chambersburg PA
CBHW050321120526
44592CB00014B/2005